LITTLE BOOK OF
NEWCASTLE UNITED

LITTLE BOOK OF
NEWCASTLE UNITED

First published in the UK in 2007

© G2 Entertainment Limited 2012

www.G2ent.co.uk

Printed and bound in China

ISBN 978-1-909040-71-7

Contents

Aitken

RIGHT Andy Aitken was a vital member of the squad that won the First Division Championship in 1904-05

SPOTTED BY NEWCASTLE United scouts in 1895 at the age of 18 while playing for Ayr Parkhouse (now Ayr United), Andrew 'Andy' Aitken (born on 27 April 1877) was a natural footballer who could play in any outfield position. His flair and ability had made him popular with local teams in his native Scotland including Elmbank and Ayr Thistle after giving up his job as a grocer's boy.

His early career got him noticed at Newton Heath and Preston, but it was for United that he signed in July 1895. Aitken's debut for United, playing at inside-left came against Loughborough Town when he scored in the 3-0 victory. Nicknamed 'Daddler', excitement grew over Aitken on the pitch with his 'in the air' skills (he could often out-jump opponents of 6'0", despite his small 5'8" frame).

Aitken was capped 14 times for Scotland between 1901-11 and proved his adaptability and versatility at Newcastle. He often turned out for Newcastle at right-half – his least favourite position – and scored 42 goals in his 349 League and FA Cup appearances for the Magpies before becoming player-manager at Middlesbrough in 1906. He later became a publican and was still in Tyneside when he died in February 1955.

Ameobi

BORN ON 12 OCTOBER 1981 IN ZARIA, Nigeria, Foluwashola 'Shola' Ameobi's career with the Black and Whites got off to a flying start when strikers Carl Cort and Alan Shearer suffered injuries. Tipped by former manager Bobby Robson as a star of the future, Ameobi was brought up in Newcastle and scored twice in 12 appearances in his first season (2000-01). Despite being tall with an aptitude for appearing ungainly, the striker's shooting and heading ability are distinctly impressive.

He scored two further goals at the start of the 2001-02 season in the Intertoto Cup and was invited to play for Nigeria's Under-21s. He opted instead to follow an international career with England and made 20 Under-21 appearances, scoring seven times.

Despite failing to make the breakthrough into the senior England squad for Euro 2004, Ameobi made his presence known at St James' Park by scoring ten goals during the 2003-04 campaign. He went on to become an important first-team player during the following season and netted seven goals in his 45 appearances. His career at United has taken off with nine goals in 30 Premiership games during 2005-06 and an England call-up is not out of the question. His career at United has seen him make more than 250 first team appearances, netting fifty goals, although he has not been able to make the breakthrough into the full England side.

BELOW Shola Ameobi scored three League goals at the start of the 2006-07 campaign before suffering a hip injury

Anderson

RIGHT John Anderson was assistant coach at St James' Park in 1992-93

BORN IN DUBLIN ON 7 November 1959, John Anderson began his football career with his home side, Stella Maris, before moving to West Bromwich Albion and Preston North End. He had also tried out for Manchester United and played Gaelic football before joining the Dublin team. He joined the Magpies in 1982 on a free transfer from Preston having been released by Gordon Lee.

The 5'11" Dubliner remained with United for ten years before a recurring ankle injury in January 1992 forced his retirement. Once established at St James' Park, Anderson proved his critics wrong and – while not blessed with finer ball skills – was to become a stalwart of the team with his hard work and determination. He also proved to be a versatile player, comfortable at full-back, in central defence or as the midfield anchor. He gained recognition and respect from his team-mates and was a firm favourite on the terraces.

Anderson made a total of 322 appearances for United scoring 15 goals. He was capped for his native Ireland 16 times and when his ankle injury made it impossible for him to don the black and white shirt anymore he moved to Berwick Rangers as manager in 1992.

Anglo-Italian Cup

THE ANGLO-ITALIAN CUP WAS A short-lived competition created by promoter Gigi Peronace in 1970 designed to generate better relations between English clubs and their Italian counterparts. Unfortunately, these games often degenerated into an ill-tempered match with players regularly sent off for fouls and brawls.

Indeed, during Newcastle's victorious 1972-73 campaign, a total of six players were dismissed during their group games against Italian opposition – four in one particularly bad-tempered meeting with Torino at St James' Park.

The competition saw four groups (two of four English and two of four Italian teams) play their continental opponents in a mini-league before the knockout phase. The Magpies kicked off with a 2-0 victory away to AS Roma in February before visitors Bologna were dispatched 1-0 a month later.

Further victories followed over Como (2-0 away) and Torino (5-1 at home) to set up a Semi-Final clash with the

other English group winners Crystal Palace. (Blackpool had finished second to Newcastle, winning all four matches but losing out with an inferior goal difference.) The Magpies triumphed in the two-legged match, drawing 0-0 at Selhurst Park before registering an emphatic 5-1 victory at home with Malcolm Macdonald scoring a hat-trick.

The Final was held in Florence in June and an own goal from Fiorentina keeper Franco Superchi together with a strike from right-back David Craig delighted the traveling supporters among the 45,000 crowd.

Attendances

THE CURRENT CAPACITY OF ST James' Park stands at 52,397 and the ever faithful Toon Army have been almost filling the ground to overflowing during recent years. The average attendance over the last three seasons has been impressive to say the least (52,032 in 2005-06, 51,844 in 2004-05 and 51,966 in 2003-04).

The club's best ever average attendance for a season, however, came in 1947-48 when an average 56,299 fans saw them clinch runner's-up position in the Second Division. This elevated the club back to the top flight for the first time in 14 years.

The ground's biggest attendance was for the visit of Chelsea for a First Division game on 3 September 1930 when a record crowd of 68,386 saw Jackie Cape score the only goal of the game as former Toon hero Hughie Gallacher finished on the losing side. The modern day (all-seated) equivalent of this is the 52,327 who watched and suffered as goals from Wayne Rooney and Ruud van Nistelrooy gave Manchester United a 2-0 victory on 28 August 2005.

Domestic Cup clashes have also brought large numbers flocking to St James' Park. Bolton Wanderers were the visitors on 27 January 1951 when 67,596 cheered the Magpies' relentless march to the Wembley Final while 49,902 witnessed a League Cup Semi-Final second leg victory over Spurs on 21 January 1976.

Ba

A COLLAPSED DEAL TO STOKE City because of a failed medical, followed by a 'pay as you play' deal at West Ham United – Demba Ba's introduction to the Premier League could hardly have been more traumatic. Add to this West Ham being relegated at the end of the season and that chances of Demba Ba becoming a cult hero anywhere must have seemed remote. Yet, in what is probably the prime example of being the right player for the right club, Demba's time at St James' Park has been an unqualified success.

Born in Sevres in France on 25 May 1985, Demba began his professional career with Rouen, neeting 22 goals in just 26 League appearances and earning a move to Mouscron in Belgium in 2006. He suffered a number of injuries that kept him out of action for some eight months but returned with a vengeance, scoring seven goals in nine appearances and also winning his first cap for Senegal. He then moved on to 1899 Hoffenheim in the German League and helped them gain promotion to the Bundesliga, where he continued his goalscoring exploits.

A planned move to Stuttgart in 2009 fell through after he failed a medical, with his Hoffenheim contract subsequently being extended. However, in January 2011 he left the club owing to a contractual dispute, agreeing a deal with Stoke that also fell through after he failed their medical. West Ham offered him a short-term deal based on appearances, with Demba repaying their faith by scoring seven goals in twelve appearances. Unfortunately it was not enough to prevent West Ham being relegated, at which point Demba

BA

RIGHT Demba Ba

left the club, with both Everton and Newcastle said to be interested.

He eventually signed for Newcastle in June 2011 and would score 16 goals in 34 appearances, a figure that might have been even higher had he not been required for duty for Senegal in the African Cup of Nations. A couple of extra goals here or there in the five matches he missed could have meant Champions League football for the Magpies. It was not to be, but his goal-scoring abilities, alongside country-man and team-mate Papiss Cisse make them an exciting duo for the future.

Babayaro

BORN ON 29 AUGUST 1978 IN Kaduna, Nigeria, defender Celestine Babayaro signed for the Magpies in January 2005 on a three and a half year contract. He played seven games for United in the 2004-05 season and followed this with 28 appearances in 2005-06.

Twice named the best young player in Belgium while with Anderlecht (in 1995 and 1996), Babayaro currently holds the record for being the youngest player to star in the Champions League at 16 years and three months.

He first came to worldwide attention with some spectacular performances for Nigeria during the 1996 Olympic Games in Atlanta where he and his African team-mates secured victory and the gold medal. (He has since captained his country at the 2000 Olympics and represented Nigeria at the 1998 and 2002 World Cups.)

Joining Chelsea for £2.25 million, he quickly adapted to the English game playing on the left-hand side in midfield or defence and won an FA Cup winner's medal in 1999-2000.

Injury and suspension saw Babayaro miss much of the 2002-03 season although he did score a spectacular goal against Middlesbrough.

A highly-rated left-sided defender or winger, Babayaro stayed at Chelsea for seven years where his speed, ball control and dangerous passing earned him the respect of opposing teams.

ABOVE Sidelined by a groin injury at the end of 2006, Celestine Babayaro was sorely missed as the Magpies struggled at the wrong end of the Premiership

Beardsley

RIGHT Peter Beardsley
finished his career
with 210 goals in 659
League games

AWARDED AN MBE FOR HIS services to football in 1995 and nick-named 'Pedro' by his team-mates, Peter Beardsley was a supreme footballer and match-winner who was adored by the fans. Born on 18 January 1961 in Longbenton, Newcastle upon Tyne, Beardsley became one of United's most prolific strikers in his two spells with the club.

Before he began his career in earnest at Newcastle (having enjoyed a spell as a teenager with the club on trial), Beardsley had successful times with both Carlisle United – under St James' Park legend Bobby Moncur – and Vancouver Whitecaps in Canada. He joined Manchester United for a short spell (playing in only one League Cup tie), before finding his way back home to the Magpies in 1983.

Known for his decisive skilful moves and his devastating creativity for both setting up and scoring goals, he quickly became a favourite with the Geordie fans. Under the inspirational guidance of captain Kevin Keegan, then in his final season as a player, Beardsley was instru-mental in helping United back into top-flight football in 1984. During the next four seasons with the Magpies, he also became a regular in the England squad and developed an exceptional partner-ship with Gary Lineker. During the World Cup Finals in Mexico in 1986, six of England's goals were famously scored by Lineker, but the seventh goal was

scored by Beardsley in the 3-0 Second Round defeat of Paraguay.

Liverpool manager Kenny Dalglish paid £1.9 million to take Beardsley to Anfield in 1987 where he won a first League title and Beardsley enjoyed the same prestige at Liverpool that he had received at United, scoring spectacular goals with his exceptional ball skills,

stamina, enthusiasm and long range shooting. After Dalglish left Liverpool in 1990, however, Beardsley found life difficult under new manager Graeme Souness. He joined Everton where he played well but he returned to Newcastle in 1993 when his old team-mate Keegan became manager and stayed with his hometown club for a further four years.

He ended his England career after 59 caps in 1996, the same year that the Magpies narrowly missed out on the Premiership title to Manchester United. He later played for Bolton Wanderers, Manchester City, Fulham and Hartlepool United before retiring from the professional game at the age of 38. During his 288 appearances for the Magpies, he rewarded the club with 111 goals. Beardsley is currently one of the coaches at Newcastle United's Youth Academy.

Bellamy

CRAIG BELLAMY JUMPED AT THE chance to join Newcastle United in the summer of 2001 for £6 million after Coventry City were relegated from the top flight. Mark Hughes, then Wales boss, had recommended Norwich City star Bellamy (with 32 goals in 83 appearances) to Coventry and he became one of the hottest strikers to join the Premiership. The Wales international had a mediocre time at Highfield Road, but made enough of an impression to convince Bobby Robson that he would be agile, spirited and skilful enough to enhance the Magpies' game and add some firepower to the club's forward line.

With lightning pace and the 2002 PFA Young Player of the Year title under his belt, Bellamy quickly established a spectacular partnership with Alan Shearer in the front line at St James' Park. Even disgrace for a caution for common assault was not enough to deter the fans and Bellamy became a popular player during his first season with the Magpies. Scoring 14 goals during his first seven months at the club – despite a staggering 11 bookings – his prospects looked bleak when a knee injury threatened

ABOVE Craig Bellamy controls the ball

to ruin his season just as United were about to launch a serious attack on Manchester United's title hopes. The injury kept Bellamy out of the team for the majority of the 2003-04 season and further legal trouble didn't help his reputation when he was found guilty of threatening, abusive and insulting language outside a nightclub in Cardiff.

He was once again in trouble during the 2004-05 season after a bitter row with Graeme Souness over whether or not he had feigned injury in order to avoid playing out of position and he was sent to Celtic on loan for the remainder of the season. The row led to other members of his team, most famously Alan Shearer, also falling out with Bellamy and it was clear that it would not be possible for him to return to Newcastle once his spell at Celtic ended.

During his brief stay in Glasgow he made 15 appearances and scored nine goals including a hat-trick against Dundee United which saw Celtic win 3-2. He joined Blackburn Rovers in July 2005, signing a four-year contract at Ewood Park and scoring 13 times in 27 League appearances. Currently the holder of 35 Welsh caps, Bellamy was snapped up by Liverpool in the summer of 2006 for a fee of £6 million.

Beresford

JOHN BERESFORD MADE HIS debut for United on 15 August 1992 in a 3-2 victory against Southend United. Born in Sheffield on 4 September 1966, he began his career as an apprentice with Manchester City in April 1983, turning professional in September that same year.

He joined Barnsley during the summer of 1986 on a free transfer before moving to Portsmouth in March 1989 for a fee of £300,000. At Fratton Park he notched up nearly 100 games including their 1992 FA Cup Semi-Final against Liverpool where he missed a spot-kick in the penalty shoot-out after the replay had finished goal-less.

Beresford had by now become a hot property with his left foot skills and gutsy determination. He almost signed for Liverpool, but a failed medical saw him head north to join Kevin Keegan's Magpies and he quickly became a favourite with the Gallowgate crowds. The fee for Beresford joining the Magpies was £650,000, and he proved consistent in his 173 appearances for the team at left-back. With his flair for attack, he was also picked for England under both Graham Taylor and Terry Venables.

Beresford joined Southampton in 1998 for £750,000 and eventually retired from playing in August 2000.

Bowyer

LEE BOWYER JOINED NEWCASTLE United after West Ham's relegation from the Premiership in May 2003. Born on 3 January 1977 in London's East End, Bowyer – a committed Hammers fan – had been keen to sign for West Ham but was unable to save them from the drop. The timing was crucial and Bowyer decided not to renew his contract. He was quickly in demand for his combative, goalscoring abilities – managers wanted him on their team and oppositions feared him.

Having signed for Charlton Athletic at the age of 17, he became the most sought after player in the summer of 1996. Bowyer chose to go to Leeds as he thought he would win more medals with the Yorkshire club – his £2.8 million fee made him Britain's most expensive teenager. He scored more than 50 goals in his 257 appearances for the club and was regularly capped for England's Under-21s (he has only won one full international cap, due in part to his much-publicised troubles in his personal life that include testing positive for cannabis at Charlton in 1994

and numerous scuffles with members of the public since).

When manager David O'Leary left Leeds in the summer of 2002, Bowyer refused to sign a new contract which was due to expire at the end of the

2002-03 season. With controversy surrounding his temperament on and off the field, Leeds decided to sell Bowyer to West Ham for a nominal fee but he only made a handful of appearances for the Hammers before his May 2003 transfer to St James' Park.

Blighted by injury during his first season with the Magpies he made just 25 appearances. His temper also continued to be a problem and, despite scoring six goals in 39 games during the 2004-05 season, he also managed to clock up three red cards and 11 yellows. Things did not improve when in April in a 3-0 defeat against Aston Villa, Bowyer had an on-field brawl with team-mate Kieron Dyer resulting in both players being sent-off. Boywer later accepted that the incident was mainly his fault and was fined six weeks' wages. After being charged with a public order offence he also had to endure a court hearing.

His career has been volatile on and off the pitch, with at one point Birmingham City supporters petitioning against the club signing him, but after Newcastle United Lee managed to win over the fans of West Ham United, Birmingham City and Ipswich Town with his all-action playing style. And those Birmingham fans even had cause to thank him as he helped the club win their first major honour in 48 year with a 2011 victory in the League Cup Final.

Bramble

BORN IN IPSWICH ON 21 JULY 1981, Titus Bramble began his career as an apprentice for his hometown club, making his League debut aged 17 at Sheffield United in December 1998. During 2000-01, the defender helped establish the side back in the Premiership with a top five finish that secured Ipswich a UEFA Cup place for the following season. Blighted by an ankle injury, his first-team appearances were not as frequent and it was only when the Magpies were satisfied that his injury was healed that they signed the young defender for £4.5 million.

Bramble signed a five-year deal with United in July 2002 after undergoing surgery on his ankle and spending several weeks on Tyneside improving his fitness. Manager Bobby Robson was keen for the defender to add some consistency and strength to the back four which had made great strides during the 2001-02 campaign. He made his debut for the Magpies in August 2002 and enjoyed his first season with the club, establishing himself as a first-team player with more than 20 appearances. His 2003-04 season was equally impressive although during his 42 appearances he did manage to clock up nine yellow cards. During the following two campaigns his form continued and he scored the only goal of the game against Chelsea in May 2006 that secured Newcastle an Intertoto place. Titus remained at Newcastle until June 2007 when he joined Wigan Athletic in order to revive his career. Three years later he returned to the North East, signing for Sunderland for £1 million.

OPPOSITE Lee Bowyer celebrates after scoring a goal

BELOW Titus Bramble celebrates with his team-mates after scoring against Chelsea in 2006

Brennan

KNOWN AS THE 'ROCK OF Tyneside', Frank Brennan is rated one of the best players to have ever played for the Magpies. His time at the club between 1946-56 saw the centre-half produce stunning football. Famous for his cool head and tough no-nonsense approach in defence, Brennan was fast and combative despite being 6'3" and wearing size 12 boots.

Born in Annathill on the outskirts of Glasgow on 23 April 1924, Brennan became the foundation of United's backline – being described as a complete defence in himself. After signing for junior club Coatbridge St Patricks, he was quickly spotted by local Scottish teams along with Wolves, eventually joining Airdrieonians in 1941. Despite his footballing success, Brennan remained working at the local pit and brickworks and regularly appeared for local side Broomfield Park during the war.

However, it was when he was chosen to play in the Victory International between Scotland and England at Hampden Park in 1946 that his profile was raised. Among the 139,000-plus crowd that day were many top managers and scouts. Brennan outplayed England legend Tommy Lawton and Newcastle made a move to sign him.

He signed for United in May 1946 for £7,500 and during his first season gained two caps for Scotland (he finished with seven in total). The following season United returned to the First Division and Brennan's popularity soared with the Geordie fans as his confident style, firm tackles and heading skills gave the entire team a boost. The 1950-51 season ended in triumph at Wembley where Brennan was praised for his dogged determination in the FA Cup Final and during the following campaign helped keep the team together when poor form threatened the club. In 1955, when United reached Wembley for a third time in five years, Brennan was nearing the end of his illustrious playing career and sadly, a number of alleged run-ins with club directors over his sports shop (which rivalled Stan Seymour's business) saw him leave under bitter circumstances rather than

the pomp and ceremony he deserved.

With his wages virtually halved, Brennan was put on the transfer list and after much media attention the directors at United took a battering. Even the TUC were involved, concerned that professional footballers were not given adequate or reasonable terms of employment. His career with the Magpies was sadly over and in 1956 he went on to spend the next six years as player-coach with North Shields before retiring to concentrate on his sports business.

Cassidy

BEFORE JOINING UNITED, Thomas Cassidy – born in Belfast on 18 November 1950 – had trials for Manchester United and tasted European football with Glentoran. He signed for United in October 1970 for a fee of £25,000.

It took Cassidy some time to win a regular place in the team but, when he did, he demonstrated his skill for creating goalscoring opportunities and his great ability with the ball. He eventually settled into midfield and, while the Magpies were qualifying for Europe and setting their sights on Wembley, Cassidy worked hard alongside Terry Hibbitt and Tommy Craig. In his 225 appearances for United, Tommy Cassidy scored a total of 28 goals.

During his ten years at St James' Park, Cassidy enjoyed a spell in South Africa playing for the Lusitano club. In 1982 he was picked to play for Ireland in the 1982 World Cup in Spain. He still ran his newsagency business as well as working on local radio while his football career flourished. He also had a spell in Cyprus, but was banned from the game by UEFA after unfounded allegations of corruption. He won 24 caps for Northern Ireland and was a Cup winner several times over.

Centenary

WITH STANLEY BEING FORMED IN November 1881, the 1981-82 campaign was the club's true centenary season and it was unspectacular to say the least. The Magpies finished ninth in the Second Division with 62 points from 42 games, a massive 26 points behind champions Luton Town.

In the FA Cup, the Magpies struggled to overcome Fourth Division Colchester United winning the Third Round replay 4-3 after the first game had ended one apiece. Their run ended in the Fourth Round with a 2-1 defeat at home to Grimsby Town while in the League Cup Third Division Fulham ended their interest in the competition with an aggregate 4-1 Second Round win.

In contrast, the season 100 years after the adoption of the Newcastle United name saw the Magpies win promotion back to the top flight after a four-year absence. The arrival of Kevin Keegan as manager had rejuvenated the team and – in the first campaign following the inauguration of the Premiership – they claimed the Division One title with a hefty 12-point margin over

runner's-up West Ham United... a far cry from the previous season when they had narrowly missed relegation to the Third Division for the first time in the club's history.

ABOVE Kevin Keegan shows his disappointment during a match

Champions League

NEWCASTLE UNITED HAVE qualified for the Champions League – UEFA's flagship European club competition – three times.

The club's best ever Premiership placing as runner's-up in 1996-97 gave them entry to the following season's competition and, having seen off Croatia Zagreb in the qualifying round, they found themselves drawn against Barcelona, Dynamo Kiev and PSV Eindhoven with home and away fixtures to fulfill.

Their opening match was home to Spanish giants Barcelona and a Faustino Asprilla hat-trick earned the Magpies a 3-2 victory. A John Beresford strike and a Golovoko own goal secured a draw in Kiev but United then went on to lose the next three games; against PSV 1-0 at home and 2-0 away and 1-0 in Barcelona. They made amends in the final group game at home to Kiev, registering a 2-0 victory courtesy of goals from John Barnes and Stuart Pearce, but it was not enough to secure a place in the Quarter-Finals.

Newcastle were again drawn with Kiev in 2002-03, along with Juventus and Feyenoord, having disposed of Zeljeznicar in qualifying, but they got off to a disastrous start losing in Kiev and Turin and at home to the Dutch side. Pride was restored, however, with three victories in the second half of the group stage. Andy Griffin scored the only goal of the game as the Italians visited St James' Park while Gary Speed and Alan Shearer netted in the 2-1 victory in Kiev. In Barcelona, a brace from Craig Bellamy and a goal from Hugo Viana ensured the Magpies' progress to the next phase in a five-goal thriller.

In the second group stage, United met Barcelona, Bayer Leverkusen and Inter Milan. Nolberto Solano scored the Magpies' only goal as Inter won 4-1 at St James' Park to end Newcastle's run of three victories in the competition. A visit to Barcelona followed and the Spaniards ran out 3-1 winners at the Nou Camp.

Shola Ameobi netted a brace and Shearer a hat-trick in the double-header

against Leverkusen to raise hopes of proceeding to the Quarter-Finals but it was not to be. A 2-2 draw in Milan preceded a 2-0 defeat at home to Barcelona and Newcastle again missed out on the knockout stages of the tournament.

The 2003-04 season saw United paired with Partizan Belgrade. Newcastle lost the away leg of the tie and won the home leg by the same 1-0 margin with extra-time failing to separate the two sides. In the ensuing penalty shoot-out, the Magpies lost 4-3 and gained entry into that season's UEFA Cup competition as consolation.

ABOVE Faustino Asprilla celebrates with a cartwheel during the Champions League match against Barcelona in 1997

Charity/ Community Shield

ORIGINALLY PLAYED BETWEEN professionals and amateur sides, the FA Charity Shield – renamed the Community Shield in 2002 – replaced the Sheriff of London Charity Shield with the first match being staged in 1908-09.

The competition evolved to be contested between the winners of the Football League (or Premiership from 1992-93 onwards) and the FA Cup. In 1959, the match was moved from the end of the season to the August before the campaign kicked off and it was FA Secretary Ted Croker who came up with the current format in 1974 whereby the winners of the two competitions play at Wembley (when available!) which increases the amount of money going to good causes.

Newcastle won the second year's fixture when they beat top non-League side Northampton Town at Stamford Bridge 2-0 with goals from Stanley 'Jack' Allan and John 'Jackie' Rutherford but this has so far been their only success. They have appeared in a further five Charity Shield matches but have lost each one: against Everton (5-3 in 1932), Tottenham Hotspur (2-1 in 1951), Manchester United (4-2 in 1952 and 4-0 in 1995) and Chelsea (3-0 in 1955).

ABOVE The British Football Association Charity Shield, 1970s

RIGHT Jackie Milburn, scorer of United's goal in the 1951 Charity Shield

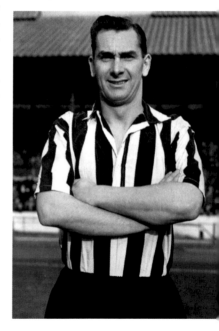

Cisse

JUST AS DEMBA BA SETTLED INTO the Newcastle side quickly and established himself as a firm fan favourite, so fellow countryman Papiss Cisse seemingly came from nowhere to attain celebrity cult status. Born in Dakar in Senegal, Papiss began his career with Douanes Dakar before transferring to France and Metz in 2005. He was sent out on loan to Cherbourg and then Chateauroux on loan before returning to Metz, where he would go on to score 36 goals in 95 League appearances.

He was sold to SC Freiburg in Germany in December 2009 and scored 37 goals in just 65 appearances, finishing second top scorer in the Bundesliga in 2010-11 and prompting several clubs to run the rule over the athletic striker. It was Newcastle who won the race for his signature, paying £8 million to ensure he linked up with Demba Ba in a potent strikeforce. Newcastle fans had to wait a while before they got to see Papiss at his best, largely because he was required for international duty at the African Cup of Nations.

When he returned it was as a

ABOVE Papiss Cisse in action for Newcastle United

man possessed, determined to show Newcastle exactly what kind of striker they had acquired. A total of 13 goals in 14 games gave him an almost perfect goal ratio, but added to this was the telepathic way he linked up with Demba Ba, giving Newcastle as potent a strike force to be found anywhere in the Premier League. Indeed, so vital has Cisse become to Newcastle, the club blocked an attempt by Senegal to name the player in the Olympic squad for 2012 – Newcastle want the player fit and ready to terrorise Premier League and European defences in the coming season.

Clark, Frank

BORN NEAR GATESHEAD ON 9 September 1943, Frank Clark has had a glittering career both on and off the pitch. With his flair for football and his head for business, Clark has contributed more to football, including 457 League and Cup games for United (the highest number by any United player in post-war football) than most.

Despite offers from West Bromwich Albion, Preston North End and Newcastle, Clark decided to concentrate on his education – doing a laboratory technician apprenticeship – and played amateur football for Crook Town, reaching Wembley in 1961 to win an FA Amateur Cup medal in a victory over Hounslow Town. Finding his way into the England amateur and youth line-ups, he also went on to captain the youth team.

His success on the amateur field once again raised interest from Newcastle and they signed him in October 1962. Unluckily, he broke his leg in a match against Liverpool Reserves in 1963, forcing him out of action but he was once again wearing the black and white

shirt by the end of 1963-64 and his sound defending skills earned him the reputation of being a reliable, consistent footballer.

He was comfortable at left-back but did play at centre-half during his last three seasons for the Magpies. Manager Joe Harvey had nothing but praise for his defender who time and time

ABOVE Frank Clark's only Newcastle United goal came in the 6-0 League Cup drubbing of Doncaster Rovers during the 1973-74 season

FAR LEFT Frank Clark jumps for the ball

ABOVE Liverpool's Steve Heighway (r) takes on Newcastle United's Frank Clark

again showed his dedication to the club despite criticism from some fans. He remained professional throughout his 13 years with United (becoming captain in 1974, succeeding Bob Moncur), and it was with some controversy that Clark left the club at the end of 1974-75 when he was given a free transfer following the resignation of Harvey.

He moved to Brian Clough's Second Division Nottingham Forest where he enjoyed five years. Forest were promoted in 1976-77 and won the First Division the following season. But the highlight of his career must surely be when Forest won the European Cup against Malmo in 1979.

He jumped at the chance to move into management that same year and took up a post with Sunderland as assistant. Having learnt much from Harvey and Clough, Clark proved his worth twice leading Leyton Orient to promotion to the Third Division in the 1980s. He also enjoyed a promotion while in the Forest hotseat (1993-96) and briefly managed Manchester City (1996-98). He became chief executive of the Managers' Association in 1992 and is currently vice chairman.

Clark, Lee

SINCE HIS RETURN TO HIS BOY-hood club, Lee Clark has played one season with the Magpies making 22 League appearances. He joined United once again after his impressive run in training and signed a short-term deal in August 2005. He is still with the club today proving his worth in midfield in the first team and helping out with the reserve team.

Born in Wallsend on 27 October 1972, Clark began his career with eight years at Newcastle coming through the youth ranks. He then moved to local rivals Sunderland for £2.5 million in the summer of 1997. He made more than 100 appearances for his new club and became captain in the absence of Kevin Ball. During this time he was also named in the PFA Division One Select XI.

Two years later, however, he moved to Fulham for £3 million. At Craven Cottage he proved his dynamic flair in midfield but it took him a while to find his feet. However, he settled back to his usual form the following season and extended his contract with Fulham for four years in August 2001.

The 2001-02 campaign proved difficult for Clark when a serious Achilles injury from the previous December meant he only played one game. He was further hampered by newspaper reports that he had said he would be moving to Glasgow Rangers – both Clark's agent and the club strongly denied the rumour. With his dedication and commitment and strong passing skills and

ABOVE Lee Clark joined the backroom staff at St James' Park at the end of the 2005-06 campaign

goalscoring ability Clark remained a favourite with both team-mates and fans at Craven Cottage.

However, things didn't get any better with a further injury to his Achilles on the opposite foot during the 2002-03 season. He made a good recovery and regained his fitness to prove that he was a valuable part of the side under Chris Coleman. Fulham and Newcastle United were drawing 1-1 on 19 April 2003 when, five minutes from the final whistle, Clark found the back of the net and secured a 2-1 victory against his boyhood club. After overcoming his Achilles problems and regaining his fitness, Clark went on to make 27 appearances during the 2003-04 season, scoring two goals, against Newcastle and Manchester United.

Fulham, however, decided his services were no longer required, releasing Clark at the end of the 2004-05 campaign and he found his way back to his former club and the black'n'white shirt. His second spell at St James' Park saw him make 22 appearances before announcing his retirement, subsequently going into management with Huddersfield Town and then Birmingham City.

Cole

BORN ON 15 OCTOBER 1971 IN Nottingham, Andrew Cole is one of the highest scoring players in the history of football with 198 Premiership goals (second only to Alan Shearer on 260). He is currently with Portsmouth having joined them from Manchester City. He has won the coveted Young Player of the Year award, the UEFA Champions League title and 15 caps for England between (1995-2000).

His career began with Arsenal in 1988 but his only appearance was as a substitute against Sheffield United during December 1990. He was loaned to Fulham the following season, scoring three goals in 13 games before being sold to Bristol City for £500,000.

He quickly became one of the hottest properties in football with his frequent goalscoring and, in February 1993, Newcastle paid a record £1.75 million to sign him. He proved his worth when he scored 12 goals in as many games helping to secure United's Division One title. When strike partner David Kelly moved to Wolves, Kevin Keegan brought in former team-mate Peter Beardsley and

the two forged a successful partnership in 1993-94. Cole scored 34 goals in 40 games as the Magpies qualified for the UEFA Cup. He went on to score a total of 41 goals breaking the club's scoring record (set by Hughie Gallacher 70 years earlier). His form continued and he scored nine goals in 18 games for United and a hat-trick against Royal Antwerp in the UEFA Cup.

OPPOSITE Lee Clark, a true Magpie with a black and white heart

BELOW Andy Cole turns to celebrate after scoring a goal against Aston Villa

Andy Cole was sold to Manchester United for £7 million in January 1995 where he scored 12 goals in his first season. He regularly partnered Eric Cantona during the 1995-96 campaign and won a Premiership winner's medal and played in United's FA Cup victory to win the club's second Double in three seasons. He was joint top scorer during 1997-98 with 18 goals but soon faced competition from Dwight Yorke, Ole Gunnar Solskjaer and Teddy Sheringham and was an integral part of the Treble-winning side the following season. He was United's top scorer again during 1999-2000, collecting his fourth title medal in five seasons but was sold to Blackburn Rovers for £8 million in 2001. He rejoined Fulham in 2004, becoming their top scorer, but refused to sign more than a 12-month contract. Having moved to Manchester City the following year, he signed a new one-year deal with the club early in June 2006. Andy would subsequently wind down his career with brief spells with Portsmouth, Birmingham City, Sunderland, Burnley and Nottingham Forest before announcing his retirement in November 2008.

Coloccini

AN EXPERIENCED AND DEPEND-able defender, Fabricio Coloccini overcame a hesitant start to his Newcastle career and has become Mr Reliable, as the manager who bought predicted. Born in Crodoba in Argentina on 22 January 1982, Fabricio made his professional debut with Boca Juniors but was soon whisked off to Europe to sign for AC Milan, the deal having been set up by Fabricio's father and result-ing in a compensation claim from Boca Juniors.

The move didn't quite work out, with Fabricio being sent out on loan to a succession of clubs before being sold to Deportivo La Coruna on a permanent basis in 2004. Over the next four years he became an established first team player, also becoming a regular in the Argentina national side. In August 2008 he was sold to Newcastle for £10 mil-lion, although he initially strug-gled to find his feet in the Premier League and was dropped on a num-ber of occasions to try and restore his confidence.

A member of the team that helped Newcastle gain promotion to the Premier League, it was his ster-ling performances in the centre of defence that laid the foundations for a season of consolidation and then a challenge at the upper reaches of the table. Appointed club captain in 2011, he has led by example ever since.

RIGHT Fabricio Coloccini in action

Cowell

ROBERT COWELL WAS BORN IN County Durham on 5 December 1922 and began his career as a solid defender, signing for the club as a youth during World War II. As an ex-miner, Bobby Cowell had some catching up to do before he made his first League appearance for the Magpies at home in a Second Division match against Newport County in 1946. The game produced the highest Football League score of 13-0. He went on to play three seasons of wartime football for United and stayed with the club for nearly ten years.

The right-back spot became his own despite tough competition from the likes of Fraser and Burke and he played in 25 FA Cup ties as Newcastle won the trophy three times.

Sadly he remained uncapped throughout his career and suffered an injury during the summer of 1955 in a friendly against Germany. It cost him his career and he quit football permanently. In 1956 he was given a testimonial which proved his popularity as more than 36,000 fans turned up to support him.

Despite appearing for more than 400 times for the Magpies, he never scored a goal but he definitely remained a firm favourite with club and fans alike.

OPPOSITE Andy Cole finished his Newcastle career with 55 goals in 70 Premiership games

BELOW The 1955 squad, (back row, l-r) Jimmy Scoular, Tom Casey, Robert Cowell, Ronnie Simpson, Jackie Milburn, Bob Stokoe, Ron Batty, Charlie Crowe (front row, l-r) Manager Duggie Livingstone, Len White, Reg Davies, Vic Keeble, Ivor Broadis, George Hannah, Bobby Mitchell, N Smith

Craig

PLAYING AT RIGHT-BACK, David James Craig signed for United in 1960 and clocked up a staggering 18 years with the club. Born in Comber, Northern Ireland on 8 June 1944, he began playing football for the Boys' Brigade before signing as an apprentice with the Magpies in August 1960. Less than two years later, in April 1962 he turned professional.

His time at St James' Park saw him judged as one of the best defenders of the game during the 1960s and 1970s and he stands as one of the club's most consistent full-backs.

He originally had trials with Scunthorpe United but, homesick, returned home to Ireland after only ten weeks. He began training as an apprentice engineer but he was soon spotted by a Newcastle scout and was invited to Tyneside. This time he settled quickly and joined fellow Irishmen Dick Keith and Alf McMichael, the club's then outstanding full-back partnership. Craig learnt a lot from Keith who gave him confidence in his abilities resulting in Joe Harvey picking him for the first team within a season and a half.

Craig showed immense dedication and his senior debut came at home in November 1963 against Cardiff City. With more than 366 appearances for United, Craig was an accomplished defender who retired in November 1978.

Davies

RONALD WYN DAVIES, UNITED'S centre-forward from 1966-71, was born in Caernarfon, Wales on 20 March 1942. Recognised as one of United's foremost stalwarts he was never considered one of the great goalscoring machines.

He joined various clubs including Caernarfon Town, Wrexham and Bolton Wanderers before signing for United in October 1966 for the fee of £80,000 but his five years helping the Magpies storm Europe was immense. United had run a close contest with Manchester City to sign Davies from Second Division Bolton where he scored 74 goals in 170 games.

His debut for United was against old rivals Sunderland. He became a firm favourite with the crowds at Gallowgate and was given the nickname 'Wyn the Leap' for his aerial acrobatics and jumping abilities. Despite never being a headline grabber, Davies was renowned for his control of the ball and managing the forward line.

As United joined the European competition, Davies' opportunistic skills enabled fellow team-mates, namely Albert Bennett and Pop Robson, to hit the back of the net. Despite his modest scoring record, Davies – a Welsh international with 34 caps – was a key factor in the club's 1968-69 European success and the fans regaled him with the chant "You've not seen nothing like the Mighty Wyn".

ABOVE Wyn Davies joined Manchester City in August 1971

Derbies

UNLIKE THE MAJORITY OF BIG clubs in England who only have one immediate neighbour competing in the same competitions (even to a certain extent in London), Newcastle United have two local rivals in Sunderland and Middlesbrough although it is with the Black Cats that the rivalry is the most intense.

Their record against Sunderland is fairly even as can be seen in the table below although the Tyne does hold the advantage over the Wear.

With Sunderland in the top flight since 1892, fans of both sides had to wait until 24 December 1898 for the first League meeting between the two clubs. Newcastle won this clash 3-2 at Roker Park with goals from outside-left Willie Wardrope and a brace from centre-forward Jock Peddie. Prior to this meeting, the two sides had met regularly in friendly matches.

The first FA Cup encounter happened in the Second Round on 12 February 1902 when a solitary

League	P	W	D	L	F	A
Newcastle United	134	51	42	41	202	202
Sunderland	134	41	42	51	202	202
FA Cup						
Newcastle United	7	3	3	1	12	5
Sunderland	7	1	3	3	5	12
League Cup						
Newcastle United	2	0	1	1	4	4
Sunderland	2	1	1	0	4	4
Play-Off						
Newcastle United	2	0	1	1	0	2
Sunderland	2	1	1	0	2	0
Anglo Scottish						
Newcastle United	1	1	0	0	2	0
Sunderland	1	0	0	1	0	2

LEFT Kieron Dyer is challenged by Danny Collins of Sunderland during a Premiership match at The Stadium of Light, April 2006

Ronald Orr strike proved to be the only goal of the game but you had to wait almost 80 years for the two sides to meet in the League Cup.

They were paired in the Second Round of the 1979-80 competition and both legs finished in 2-2 draws. Ian Davies and Peter Cartwright scored at Roker with Alan Shoulder and Stuart Boam netting in the home leg. Much to their chagrin, the Magpies lost this encounter following the dreaded penalty shoot-out.

Their FA Cup meetings frequently end in draws with replays being required to find a victor. In a Fourth Round clash in 1908-09, the first game was drawn 2-2 at St James' Park before United went on to register a 3-0 victory at their opponent's ground. In 1912-13, a second replay was required after the first two Fourth Round games were drawn 0-0 and 2-2. This time, it was the Roker Park outfit who emerged victorious at the home of their rivals.

Other notable derbies over the years include the First Division match on 5 December 1908 when Sunderland hammered Newcastle 9-1 at St James' Park. The Black and Whites got their

revenge for this humiliating scoreline when they too doled out a drubbing, beating the Black Cats 6-1

on 9 October 1920. Stan Seymour, Andy Smailes (2), Neil Harris (2) and Ted Ward were the scorers in this Division One clash. United repeated this scoreline in their 1955 Boxing Day clash at Roker Park.

Dyer

RIGHT Injury again
hampered Kieron Dyer's
2006-07 campaign
with his first League
appearance coming in
November

MIDFIELDER KIERON DYER began his career in football for his hometown team Ipswich Town, where he was born on 29 December 1978. Following several injuries, Dyer has failed to win a regular place in the starting line-up for England, despite being regularly capped. He first signed for Ipswich as a 17-year-old trainee in 1996 and was picked for the first team during his first season.

Wanting to further his international prospects, Dyer requested a transfer to a bigger club in 1999 and in July was sold to Newcastle for £6.5 million. He scored against rivals Sunderland in his first match as United lost 2-1. He made his England debut not long after arriving on Tyneside although he was no stranger to the international scene having represented his country at Youth, Under-21 and 'B' levels. He went on to play for England in the 2002 World Cup and Euro 2004.

Despite suffering with injuries, his skill and pace are renowned throughout the Premiership. Unfortunately, at the beginning of the 2005-06 season Dyer was again hampered by injury and did not return to first-team action until February 2006. Kieron remained at Newcastle until the summer of 2007, subsequently going on to play for West Ham, Ipswich and QPR.

Eastham

BORN ON 23 SEPTEMBER 1936 IN Blackpool, George Eastham signed for United in May 1956 for £9,000. Football was in his family; his father had played for Bolton Wanderers and England while older brother Harry had played for Liverpool and Newcastle during World War II. His family moved to Ireland while he was a teenager and while training to become a joiner he had trials with both Blackpool and Bolton.

He was spotted by Newcastle scout Bill McCracken who brought the 19-year-old to Tyneside. His debut came against Luton Town on 6 October 1956 and he went on to score 34 goals in 129 appearances for the Magpies. He argued against the contract system, wanting to play for the club of his choice and a major dispute ensued. With the backing of the Players' Union, he took Newcastle United to court

ABOVE George Eastham playing for England

where he won a litigation battle. The legal processes were not finalised until 1963 after he had been allowed leave the Magpies.

He joined Arsenal and made 223 appearances for the Gunners. Both George Eastham senior and junior are the only father and son to have played for England, and Eastham junior was picked for both the 1962 and 1966 World Cup squads. Eventually he emigrated to South Africa while back home he was awarded an OBE in 1975 for his services to football.

Elliott

BORN IN GOSFORTH, NEWCASTLE upon Tyne on 25 December 1973 and growing up supporting his local team, it was only natural that Robert Elliott should end up playing for the Magpies. He had trials with Southampton and Manchester United and played for the England Youth and Under-18 teams but it was the support of Ossie Ardiles that paved the way for a career in professional football. The arrival of Kevin Keegan developed Elliott's game and his versatility (at left-back, in central defence and midfield) began to shine.

Robbie Elliott signed for United as a 17-year-old in 1989, turning professional in April 1991. He became an accomplished footballer under Keegan and later Kenny Dalglish, but was in tough competition with John Beresford for the left-back role. Eventually Dalglish suggested that Elliott try midfield and he went on to score seven goals in 16 games.

He signed for Bolton Wanderers in 1997-98 but ran into bad luck when he broke his leg in his first game. Despite enjoying his time at the Reebok Stadium, the lure of home and the North East

proved too much for Elliott and he was delighted to receive a call from Bobby Robson in 2001 taking him back to St James' Park. Robbie's spell at St James' Park saw him make a further 66 League appearances for the club before moving on to local rivals Sunderland, subsequently finishing his playing career with Leeds United and Hartlepool.

European Cup Winners' Cup

ENTRY INTO THE EUROPEAN CUP Winners' Cup is automatic for those teams that win the equivalent of their country's domestic FA Cup. Newcastle, however, qualified for the 1998-99 competition courtesy of the fact that FA Cup winners Arsenal – who had beaten the Magpies 2-0 at Wembley the previous May – had already won a place in the Champions League so their place was given to the losing Finalists.

United were drawn against Yugoslavian side Partizan Belgrade, who had come through the qualifying round with a 3-0 aggregate win over Dinamo Batumi of Georgia. The tie began well, with Alan Shearer and Greek central defender Nikos Dabizas scoring the goals that earned their club a 2-1 victory at St James' Park.

Unfortunately, the return leg was not as successful as Newcastle lost 1-0 as the home side scored the only goal of the game to level the tie at 2-2. Under UEFA rules, Belgrade went through to the next round because they had scored an away goal at St James' Park but they found Italian giants Lazio impossible to overcome come and went out 3-2 on aggregate.

It would prove to be the last season that UEFA ran the European Cup Winners' Cup.

BELOW Nikolaos Dabizas and Robert Lee celebrate during the European Cup Winners' Cup against Partizan Belgrade in 1998

FA Cup

NEWCASTLE UNITED DOMINATED the FA Cup during the early years of the 19th century, appearing in five Finals in seven years between 1905-1911 but only winning once.

Manager Frank Watt led the team to Crystal Palace in front of 101,117 for their first outing in an FA Cup Final in 1905. Unfortunately, United were unable to overcome Aston Villa who won with two Harry Hampton goals. The following season saw them paired with Everton but the Toffees claimed the trophy with Sandy Young scoring the only goal of the game in the 75th minute. The Magpies were back at Crystal Palace two years later and, at 2-0 down, Jimmy Howie scored to give the Newcastle faithful hope against Wolves but the

game eventually finished 3-1.

Their Crystal Palace jinx continued in 1910, drawing the Final 1-1 with Burnley. In the replay at Goodison Park, however, United finally claimed their first FA Cup when two goals from Albert Shepherd gave them a 2-0 victory. They fell at the last hurdle when attempting to defend their crown the following season, drawing 0-0 with Bradford City but losing the Old Trafford replay 1-0.

There then followed a run of five Final victories: the first, in 1924, saw Newcastle gain revenge on Aston Villa for their 1905 defeat when Neil Harris and Stan Seymour netted to give the Magpies a

2-0 victory. This was followed eight years later with a 2-1 triumph over Herbert Chapman's Arsenal, Jack Allen scoring both United's goals.

The St James' Park outfit enjoyed a hat-trick of FA Cup wins in the 1950s. Toon hero Jackie Milburn scored twice as Stanley Matthews' Blackpool were beaten 2-0 in 1951 while the following year George Robledo netted the only goal of the game as Arsenal were once again the victims. Newcastle's last FA Cup triumph to date came in 1955 when Milburn, Bobby Mitchell and George Hannah scored one apiece to see off the challenge of Manchester City.

The Magpies have been losing Finalists on three other occasions since, the first in 1974 when Bill Shankly's Liverpool ended their dream by winning 3-0 at Wembley... a certain Mr Keegan netting twice for the Reds!

Two more Cup Final appearances followed as the 20th century drew to a close. In 1998, Arsenal – on their way to the Double – won 2-0 after Shearer and Dabizas had hit the woodwork and the following season Newcastle fell victim to Manchester United by a similar scoreline as the Old Trafford side secured the second stage of their unique Treble.

FA Premiership

FEW COULD HAVE PREDICTED how successful Newcastle United's first season in the Premiership would turn out to be. With Andy Cole topping the scoring charts with an astounding 34 goals from 40 games, the Magpies set a new Premiership record for the number of goals scored in a season with 82. (This would stand until eclipsed by the 97 Manchester United scored in 1999-2000.)

Kevin Keegan had brought Peter Beardsley back to Tyneside in a bargain £1.5 million transfer and the 30-year-old forged a superb partnership with Cole to lift United to third place behind Manchester United and Blackburn Rovers.

The 1994-95 season started impeccably with United remaining undefeated after 11 games – winning nine – and starting to open up a gap at the top of the Premiership. Unfortunately, the Magpies were unable to maintain this momentum and faded as the season drew to a close, finishing in sixth position with 20 wins and 12 draws from their 42 games.

The following campaign proved to be an even closer fought affair, with Newcastle pushing Manchester United all the way to the wire. With the Black and Whites enjoying a 12-point advantage at one stage in the season, the pressure was such that Alex Ferguson implied that opponents tried harder against his Old Trafford side than against Newcastle and this triggered an emotional response from Keegan on live television after a particularly difficult victory over Leeds United. As it was, the Red Devils claimed the crown four points ahead of Newcastle.

With record £15 million signing Alan Shearer – who chose St James' Park over Old Trafford – banging in 25 goals in 31 games during the 1996-97 season, Newcastle again finished runners-up to Manchester United. But the biggest shock of the campaign was when Keegan announced his resignation in January 1997 and was replaced by Kenny Dalglish. This success proved to be a false dawn, however, as United then endured four seasons of mid-table mediocrity before once again finding the right blend of players to challenge for honours.

Bobby Robson led the Magpies to three top five finishes as the 21st century dawned. They ended the 2001-02 campaign in fourth place but went one better the following season with only Manchester United and Arsenal above them. Fifth position a year later preceded a disappointing start to the 2004-05 season that saw Robson sacked after just four games to be replaced by Graeme Souness.

Various managerial changes saw Sam Allardyce controversially leave the club in January 2008. After several rumours of potential contenders, Kevin Keegan made a sensational, dramatic return to the club on the 16th January 2008. The club suffered relegation at the end of the 2008-09 season but bounced back the following season as champions and ensured a return to Europe at the end of the 2011-12 season after finishing in fifth place in the table.

Famous Fans

WITH A CLUB AS BIG AS NEWCASTLE United, it is no surprise that there are plenty of well-known celebrities who have black and white running through their veins.

Probably the most well-known famous fans are TV duo Ant and Dec. The pair who host their own Saturday night entertainment show, first came to prominence as PJ and Duncan on *Byker Grove* (a children's programme set in the Byker district of Newcastle upon Tyne).

Other high profile supporters include Prime Minister Tony Blair; television stars Donna Air (*Big Breakfast*), Gabby Logan (*On The Ball*) and Jack Ryder (Jamie Mitchell in *EastEnders*); actor/singers Robson Green (*Soldier Soldier*) and Jimmy Nail (*Auf Wiedersehen, Pet*); pop star Sting (*the Police*) and from the world of sport former World Champion boxer Chris Eubank and darts commentator Sid Waddell.

RIGHT Robson Green

BELOW TV presenters Ant McPartlin (l) and Declan Donnelly

Ferdinand

BORN ON 8 DECEMBER IN NOTTING Hill, London in 1966, Les Ferdinand was a powerful centre-forward famed for his ability in the air. His career began in non-League football with Southall and Hayes, but he was spotted by Queens Park Rangers and signed for £15,000 in June 1986.

Making his England debut in 1994, he had a prolific career with QPR, scoring 90 goals in 183 games. He was capped 17 times for England and scored five goals. During his time at Rangers, he was loaned to Brentford (1987-88) and Turkish team Besiktas (1988-89).

He joined United in June 1995 for a record £6 million and scored 29 goals as the club narrowly missed out on the Premiership title. He set up a strike partnership with Alan Shearer that was just what both club and country needed.

Highly thought of by the fans, Ferdinand scored 50 goals in 84 games for the Magpies. He was a player whose pace, aerial ability and striking prowess earned him the nickname 'Sir Les'. Ferdinand went on to sign for Spurs (1997), West Ham (2002), Leicester (2003), Bolton Wanderers (2004) and Reading (2005), before committing himself to non-contract terms with Watford as part-time player and coach.

BELOW Les Ferdinand was awarded the MBE in 2005

Gallacher

HUGHIE GALLACHER PLAYED centre-forward for United between 1925-30 and it is argued that he was the best of all time. Born in Bellshill, Lanarkshire on 2 February 1903, he signed for United in December 1925 from Airdrieonians (whom he joined in May 1921) for £6,500.

A playboy off the pitch, Gallacher became a cult figure for the fans on Tyneside and when he captained the team to the League title in 1927, scoring a record 39 goals in just 41 games, he could do no wrong. He eventually finished with a staggering 463 goals in 624 senior matches.

Despite his small frame and height (he was only 5' 5"), Gallacher was a nightmare for opposition defences with his ability to shoot with either foot and dribbling skills. He was also renowned for losing his patience and temper. He was often in trouble with referees, directors and, less often, the police.

His relationship with the directors at St James' Park was volatile and he was eventually sold to Chelsea in 1930. Gallacher also scored a total of 23 goals for Scotland in only 20 games. After a series of personal problems, Gallacher committed suicide in Gateshead on 11 June 1957.

Gascoigne

FROM HIS BEGINNINGS WITH United in 1980 as an apprentice, Paul Gascoigne showed outstanding promise and displayed the qualities of a natural born footballer. He went on to become one of the country's leading players with a style both on and off the pitch that made him one of Tyneside's most famous sons and a household name.

Born in Dunston, Gateshead on 27 May 1967, Gazza turned professional in May 1985 – having displayed his incredible skill and promise with United's FA Youth Cup victory – and stayed with the Magpies until his move to Tottenham Hotspur in July 1988.

It was during his time at Spurs that he was to make his name both on and off the pitch with just about everyone, it seemed, wanting something from him. With his exuberant personality and flair he was constantly in the media and even advertised Brut on television. However, there was some frustration back home on Tyneside – he'd been the club's biggest discovery – and he'd had to leave his Geordie roots to find the superstardom that he obviously enjoyed.

In midfield, he possessed superb vision and was a real hot-shot with extensive passing and dribbling skills. He was the footballing phenomenon of the 1990s. At St James' Park, Gazza had taken over the midfield mantle from Chris Waddle and Peter Beardsley, sometimes showing his inexperience

BELOW Paul Gascoigne attempts to control the ball

but also his potential. In his 109 appearances for the Black and Whites he scored 25 goals. He won 57 England caps and claimed the coveted BBC Sports Personality of the Year title following his World Cup Semi-Final tears in 1990.

It was under Terry Venables at Spurs that Gazza really flourished, but after a reckless tackle and a cruciate knee ligament injury – from which it took a while to recover – in the 1991 FA Cup Final, Gazza found himself in a record £8.5 million transfer to Lazio. Due to his recuperation and fitness however, the deal – by then for the reduced fee of £5.5 million – fell through until the following year. He enjoyed three years with Glasgow Rangers (1995-98) and brief stints at Middlesbrough and Everton before joining Burnley then Gansu in China and eventually Boston United. He tried his hand at management with short spells at Algarve United (Portugal) and Conference side Kettering Town in 2005.

Despite his reputation for being rash and temperamental, Gazza will certainly always be one of the Geordie greats whose huge contribution to football will never be forgotten.

Gillespie

MIDFIELDER KEITH GILLESPIE was born in Larne, County Antrim, Northern Ireland on 18 February 1975. He began his career with Manchester United where he struggled to establish himself as a first-team player despite success in the 1992 Youth Cup-winning side. He was loaned to Wigan Athletic in 1993-94 before signing for the Magpies in January 1995 in a transfer deal which saw Andy Cole move in the opposite direction to Old Trafford.

Settling quickly at St James' Park, Gillespie soon showed an already impressed Kevin Keegan that the Northern Ireland international was well worth signing. During his five seasons and 143 appearances for the Magpies he scored 13 goals and played in 15 European ties, famously coming off the bench to set up two goals for Faustino Asprilla against Barcelona in 1997-98.

He joined Blackburn Rovers for the 1998-99 campaign and stayed for two seasons before joining Wigan Athletic for a second time in 2000-01, once again on loan. He was back, later that season, at Ewood Park where he made

another 138 appearances (scoring six goals) before moving to Leicester City for the 2003-04 season. Gillespie signed for Sheffield United in August 2005 and later played for Charlton, Bradford City, Glentoran and Darlington before returning to Ireland to play for Longford Town. Gillespie won 86 caps for Northern Ireland during his career.

ABOVE Keith Gillespie helped United reach the 1998 FA Cup Final but was left out of the Wembley showpiece

OPPOSITE Paul Gascoigne with his award during the Sports Review Of The Year ceremony, 1990

Ginola

CHARISMATIC FRENCHMAN David Ginola joined the Magpies' midfield in a debut against Coventry City on the 19 August 1995. Born in Gassin, Cote d'Azur, on 25 January 1967, Ginola's signing for United filled the Toon Army with expectation.

His career began in the south of France, establishing himself with Paris St-Germain between 1991-95. As a creative attacking player, Ginola earned the nickname 'Il Magnifique' in France, despite only being capped for the national side 17 times.

Ginola's balance and poise along with his tremendous technique and style on the ball enhanced his reputation when he arrived from the other side of the English Channel having clocked up 400 senior appearances. Club and fans alike at St James' Park hoped that the 'pin up' (he also had a contract with Italian fashion house Cerutti) would turn the Magpies into a trophy-winning side.

Known for his ability to use both feet for crossing and passes, opposing players needed to work together to stop the midfielder from racing away with the ball. In more than 70 appearances for Newcastle between 1995-97, he scored seven goals before joining Spurs (1997-2000), Aston Villa (2001-02) and Everton (2002). He was voted both the PFA's and FWA's Footballer of the Year in 1999.

Given

HAVING BEEN INSTRUMENTAL IN Newcastle United's climb up the table following the team's poor start to the 2005-06 season, goalkeeper Shay Given signed a new five-year deal with the Magpies for the start of the 2006-07 campaign. The Republic of Ireland international, born on 20 April 1976 in Lifford, dominated the scene in 2004-05 – winning the FA Cup Quarter-Final Player of the Round – and kept 15 clean sheets in 52 games. Disappointingly, his efforts to help his national side qualify for the 2006 World Cup did not pay off, despite his talent and determination.

As a superb shot-stopper, Given is rarely beaten in one-on-one situations, earning him a reputation as one of the best goalkeepers in the Premiership. His efforts for Ireland during the 2002 World Cup saw his team reach the Second Round, where he made a big impression. Ireland, however, eventually lost on penalties to Spain.

He was ever-present for United during the 2001-02 season and was also voted into the PFA's Premiership Team of the Season that campaign. Given

became the Magpies' most capped player in April 2003 after fighting off challenges for his first-team place and made his 200th appearance for United during 2003-04. His consistent form for both his club and national team has cemented his well-earned reputation of being the best and he set a new record of 140 consecutive Premiership appearances, although this was later overtaken.

He began his career for Lifford Celtic at the age of 14 and played in the FAI's Junior Cup against Dundalk, losing 1-0. However, his talents were obvious to all and he was invited to join Celtic on a pre-season tour of Ireland, aged just 15, signing for them a year later. In 1994 he joined Blackburn Rovers where Kenny Dalglish was instrumental in his development.

Finding it impossible to dislodge England international Tim Flowers as first choice keeper at Ewood Park, and having been on loan to both Swindon Town and Sunderland, Given followed Dalglish to Newcastle in 1997, costing £1.5 million, where his appearances for the first team allowed him to further develop his skills and enhance his international career. He made his debut for the Magpies in August 1997 and would go on to make 344 League appearances for the club, earning a reputation as one of the best 'keepers in the division. A £7 million switch in February 2009 took him to Manchester City, where he would make 50 appearances before being dislodged as the club's first choice. He subsequently joined Aston Villa in 2011.

Gullit

BORN ON 1 SEPTEMBER 1962 IN Amsterdam, Ruud Gullit became manager in 1998 following a successful playing career with Haarlem, Feyenoord, PSV Eindhoven, Sampdoria (twice), AC Milan (twice) and Chelsea which spanned 19 years. He was also a Dutch international with 66 caps, making his debut against Switzerland in 1981.

He rose to the challenge of becoming player-manager when Glenn Hoddle was given the England manager's job in 1996. Just one year later, Gullit was the first non-British and youngest manager to win the FA Cup with a 2-0 victory against Middlesbrough. But negotiations over his new contract didn't go well and Gullit joined Newcastle in 1998, taking over the reigns from Kenny Dalglish. Despite United making an FA Cup Final appearance in his first season, the start of the following campaign was poor and a well-publicised disagreement with Alan Shearer and a falling out with Robert Lee did little to enhance his chances of survival.

Gullit resigned as manager after only five games of the 1999-2000 campaign following a home defeat to Sunderland. He took over as manager of Feyenoord at the start of 2004-05 but resigned after one season when his team failed to win any trophies. He is now a television pundit.

BELOW Ruud Gullit becomes Newcastle United manager in 1998

Hannah

RIGHT George Hannah, an FA Cup winner in 1955

GEORGE HANNAH, BORN IN Liverpool on 11 December 1928, looked rather frail on the pitch at only nine and a half stone when he signed for United in September 1949 – making his debut at home in a match to Manchester City. But despite his frame, Hannah was a favourite with the fans with his excellent ball skills and entertaining play between 1952-55.

He began his career as an amateur for Everton and soon proved his slick style of play. He was spotted along with Alf McMichael playing for Linfield in Ireland while serving with the Royal Ulster Rifles. He was not really an automatic choice when he joined the Magpies, however, his integral part in the FA Cup – scoring a goal in a victory over Manchester City at Wembley – might have led to an England cap.

Renowned for being liable to find the back of the net, Hannah eventually scored 43 goals for the Magpies during his 177 appearances for the club.

His career lasted until he was almost 40 years old. He moved to Lincoln City in September 1957 for a fee of £5,000 before joining Manchester City just a year later. He later joined Notts County before finally settling at Bradford City, from where he retired in May 1966. George Hannah died in Sale, Cheshire on 5 May 1990.

Harvey

JOE HARVEY IS THE LONGEST serving United manager (1962-75) and is still the last manager to win a major trophy with the club. Born in Edlington, near Doncaster on 11 June 1918, Harvey also played at right-half for the club between 1945-55, making his debut at home against Barnsley on 5 January 1946.

As a player, Harvey, at 6' 0" was lean, tall and strong who performed well under pressure. He had developed his skills during World War II with 126 games for Bradford City, and as a former sergeant-major had a no-nonsense approach to the game which proved integral for any team he played for and was renowned for bellowing instructions all over the pitch whenever possible. He played for many clubs during this time, often as a war guest including: Bradford Park Avenue (1936, 1941-42), Wolves (1936), Bournemouth (1937), Bradford City (1938), Watford (1942-43), Aldershot (1943-45), York City (1943-45), Hartlepool United (1944-45), Aberdeen and Dundee United.

He eventually signed for United for a fee of £4,250 in October 1945. As captain, Harvey twice took the Magpies to FA Cup victory in 1951 and 1952 before becoming player-trainer in June 1953. A year later he retired from playing to take over as trainer full time. He then had spells as trainer for Crook Town and Barrow before taking over as manager with Workington in June 1957. But the lure of United was too much and he began his managerial role with the Magpies in June 1962.

ABOVE Joe Harvey with the FA Cup trophy which his team won for the second year running

ABOVE Joe Harvey leads out Newcastle for the 1951 FA Cup Final at Wembley

He rejoined United after they had suffered relegation from the First Division, having failed to beat Charlie Mitten to the post previously. However, by 1965, the club had re-established themselves, winning the Second Division. After qualifying for the Inter-Cities Fairs Cup in 1969, the club won the competition at the first time of asking.

With star players such as Malcolm Macdonald, Wyn Davies and Jimmy Smith, Harvey brought the club back from obscurity although he was disappointed that having made the Final of the 1974 FA Cup against Liverpool the team lost by 3-0 and Joe Harvey missed his chance of seeing his club win a major domestic trophy.

Harvey remained a stalwart of the club until his death in Newcastle on 24 February 1989 – he had given most of his adult life to the cause of Newcastle United and was given a belated testimonial at St James' Park in 1977 for nearly 40 years' service.

Hibbitt

MIDFIELDER TERRY HIBBITT, BORN on 1 February 1947 in Bradford, adopted the North East as his home. He started out as an apprentice for Leeds United in April 1963 and turned professional 20 months' later. Hibbitt scored on his Leeds debut and won an Inter-Cities Fairs Cup winners' medal in 1968 with the First Division title following a year later. He signed for the Magpies in August 1971 for £30,000.

Hibbitt – along with new centre-forward Malcolm Macdonald – became a driving force and added greater depth to the team. Renowned for his quick left foot, Hibbitt's partnership with Macdonald took off as the two players complemented each other's game with Hibbitt's accurate long-balls perfectly suited to Macdonald's pace.

Despite his small frame, Hibbitt played competitively and his fiery character and determination won the hearts of the fans. He left for Birmingham City in September 1975 but was back at St James' Park in April 1978 in an exchange with Stewart Barraclough before persistent injury saw him retire in June 1981.

He joined Gateshead as player-coach later that year and eventually settled in Ponteland on the outskirts of Newcastle before his untimely death from cancer at the age of 46 on 5 August 1994.

BELOW Terry Hibbitt scored 18 goals in 292 appearances

Howie

JAMES HOWIE MADE A TOTAL OF 237 appearances as inside-right for the Black and Whites between 1903 and 1910. He scored 82 goals and was recognised as one of the best inside-rights of his era, pre-World War I.

Born in Galston, Ayrshire on 19 March 1878, he began his career with Galston Athletic and Kilmarnock before joining Kettering Town in 1901. The following year he signed for Bristol Rovers before finally signing for United in May 1903 for a £300 fee. He made his debut for the club in a home match against Aston Villa on 2 September 1903. The charismatic Scot was known as 'Gentleman Jim' and showed much finesse during his seven full seasons with the Magpies.

Despite not being particularly fast, Howie had exceptional ball skills, especially when dribbling. His partnership with Jackie Rutherford on the right wing is accredited with seeing United claim three Championship wins and the club's first ever FA Cup trophy.

He was capped three times for Scotland between 1905-08 and left for Huddersfield Town in 1910. Following

his retirement from playing, he managed Queens Park Rangers (1913-20) and Middlesbrough (1920-23) before settling in London as a tobacconist. He died in January 1963.

Intertoto Cup

NEWCASTLE UNITED HAVE PARTIC-ipated in three Intertoto Cup campaigns in an attempt to secure European qualification after missing out on an automatic spot in the League.

The first in 2001-02 saw Sporting Lokeren convincingly beaten 4-0 in Belgium, with Shola Ameobi grabbing two goals to make the return leg a formality. In the St James' Park match, Craig Bellamy scored the only goal of the game to send the Magpies through 5-0 on aggregate.

German side 1860 Munich were the opponents in the second qualifying round and goals from Nolberto Solano (2) and Aaron Hughes gave United a 3-2 advantage in the away leg. Solano was again on the scoresheet in the return tie, along with Lomano Lua Lua and Gary Speed as the Magpies ran out 3-1 winners to set up a clash with Troyes.

United fought out a creditable goal-less draw in France but were unable to find the winning goal at St James' Park as the match ended 4-4 and Troyes progressed on the away goals rule.

The 2005-06 campaign began in style against FK ZTS Dubnica with a 5-1 aggregate victory over the Slovakians. Deportivo La Coruna proved too strong in the next round, registering 2-1 wins in both Spain and Newcastle. The Magpies learned from their mistake, however, and ensured their entry into the following season's UEFA Cup with a 4-1 aggregate victory over Lillestrom.

Internationals

GOALKEEPER SHAY GIVEN BECAME Newcastle United's most capped player on 30 April 2003 when he made his 41st appearance for the Republic of Ireland. The previous record had been set by left-back Alf McMichael who turned out 40 times for Northern Ireland in the 1950s. Given has since taken his tally to 76 caps.

Of course, Newcastle have supplied international teams with more than players adept at preventing the opposition from scoring and can boast a long tradition of strikers – including Alan Shearer, Malcolm Macdonald and Jackie Milburn – who have pulled on an England shirt.

Milburn netted on his debut, a 6-2 victory over Northern Ireland on 9 October 1948, and went on to win 13 caps and scored ten goals. Macdonald had the distinction of scoring five goals in one game when England beat Cyprus 5-0 in a European Championship qualifier on 16 April 1975.

Shearer, of course, will need no introduction to today's generation of England fans and registered 30 goals

in 63 appearances before he retired from international football at the age of 30 after Euro 2000. He is currently equal fifth with Tom Finney and Nat Lofthouse in the all-time England scoring table behind Bobby Charlton (49), Gary Lineker (48), Jimmy Greaves (44) and Michael Owen (36).

Jenas

BORN IN NOTTINGHAM ON 18 February 1983, Jermaine Jenas slotted very comfortably into United's midfield. The club paid Nottingham Forest £5 million for a man who has become one of English football's hottest properties.

He made his Forest debut in a 1-0 defeat by Sheffield United in the Third Round of the FA Cup in January 2001. Cash-strapped Forest had been forced to use young players who had come up through the ranks, giving Jenas a lucky break.

Bobby Robson brought Jenas on with 16 minutes to go for his first game with Newcastle with his full debut taking place against local rivals Sunderland on 2 February 2002. It was one of the club's toughest fixtures, however, the Magpies won 1-0. The 2002-03 season saw the young player establish himself in the first team, scoring seven goals, while he also won his first full cap for England in a 3-1 defeat to Australia.

He continued to impress and by May 2004 had earned six caps for England (although he was not picked for Euro 2004 he did make the squad for Germany 2006). His form continued throughout the 2004-05 season and on transfer deadline day signed for Tottenham Hotspur for a £7 million fee.

ABOVE Jermaine Jenas described playing for Newcastle as "living in a goldfish bowl", because of the huge fanbase and media attention

Keegan

JOSEPH KEVIN KEEGAN is one of football's greatest players of all time. Born on 14 February 1951 in Armthorpe, Yorkshire, he is both a former England and Newcastle United manager and player. However, after eight years of retirement in Spain after his playing days finished with a two-year spell at St James' Park, Keegan returned to Newcastle as manager where he is known as the 'Geordie Messiah', leading the club to become First Division champions in 1993 following the formation of the Premiership.

While with the Magpies, Keegan finished runners-up to Manchester United in 1996. Despite becoming director of football in 1994 in a deal that should have seen him with United for the next ten years, Keegan resigned from the club in January 1997. His most prolific sign-ing during his time with the Magpies must be star striker Alan Shearer for a record £15 million from Blackburn Rovers. His most famous falling out also came during his time at the club when Sir Alex Ferguson stated that Premiership sides tried much harder against Manchester United than they did against Newcastle. Keegan was furious and gave an emotional interview on Sky Sports in response. At the time, United had lost their 12-point lead in the Premiership and it was Fergie's team that eventually won the title.

Keegan moved to Second Division Fulham and was appointed chief operating officer before taking over the managerial reigns. Despite winning the Second Division title, Keegan decided to take up the post of England coach in an unpopular move with Fulham fans in February 1999.

On 24 May 2001 he took up the post of manager for First Division Manchester City where they went on to become Champions in his first season. Things went well at the club until the 2003-04 season when relegation beckoned. He was heavily criticised for his choice of players and on 10 March 2005 he decided to retire.

As a player, Keegan was known to be fast and brave and it was Scunthorpe United that were the first to offer him terms. He moved to Liverpool in the summer of 1971, and after 100 goals and 323 appearances for Liverpool Kevin Keegan joined Hamburg SV where he went on to become a worldwide superstar and twice received the coveted title of European Footballer of the Year before signing for Southampton and Newcastle United.

Keegan announced his retirement from management in 2005. He did however take tyneside by surprise in January 2008 when after much speculation he made a remarkable return to

Kits

NEWCASTLE UNITED HAVE BEEN playing in black and white stripes for more than 110 years but the origins of the kit design remain clouded in mystery.

One theory is that it stems from the black and white habit worn by staunch supporter and local monk Father Dalmatius Houtmann while another suggests that magpies nesting in St James' Park's old Victorian Stand gave the players the idea of adopting a similar colour scheme. A third and possibly more plausible theory is that the colours stem from the 17th century Duke of Newcastle whose coat of arms boasted three white stags on a black background and whose volunteer army was kitted out all in black apart from their white shirts.

Whatever the truth behind the decision, it is a far cry from the all red strip and change kit of red and white stripes worn by predecessors Newcastle East End. Club directors decided on the new colours on 2 August 1894 to avoid colour clashes with opposing teams.

With different kit manufacturers sup-

ABOVE Bill McCracken in the 1912 kit

ABOVE RIGHT Bryan Robson wearing the 1970 shirt

BELOW RIGHT Albert Luque wearing the kit in 2006

plying the shirts over the years, the width of the stripes has changed and individuality has been maintained by varying the away and third-choice strips.

Krul

TIM WAS ASSOCIATED WITH RAS and ADO Den Haag as a youngster but signed his first professional contract with Newcastle United in the summer of 2005, seen a an exciting prospect for the future. Born in The Hague in the Netherlands on 3 April 1988, Tim was known as Bakkers Handen whilst at RAS, which translates as baker's hands and reflects how safe he is in goal.

Sent out on loan to Falkirk and Carlisle during his early days at Newcastle, Tim grasped the opportunity of gaining first team experience with both hands and returned to Newcastle as deputy to Steve Harper following Shay Given's sale to Manchester City. He made his first team League appearance in September 2010 when Harper was injured midway through a Tim's performances were of such quality that even when fit again, Harper was unable to dislodge the youngster from the side. With experience has come stature, with Tim managing to keep fifteen clean sheets during the 2011-12 season, the foundations of the club's charge up the League table.

LEFT Tim Krul in action for his national team

Having been capped for Holland at Under 17 level in 2005, the national side kept tabs on him during his early formative years at Newcastle, finally rewarding him with a full cap in 2011. He has since added two further caps to that tally and with age very firmly on his side seems certain to add to that total in the years to come. As well as keeping further clean sheets for Newcastle.

LAWRENCE

RIGHT Jimmy Lawrence, in the days before goalkeepers were required to wear a different coloured shirt

Lawrence

JAMES LAWRENCE WAS ONE OF the first characters in Newcastle United's history and enjoyed a staggering 18 years at St James' Park as goalkeeper between 1904-22. As first-team goalkeeper for 14 straight seasons, he was on top form with his consistent style and made a record 432 League appearances for the senior side during the Edwardian era. His overall number of appearances totalled 507 by the time he left the club in 1922.

Born in Glasgow on 16 February 1885, Jim Lawrence played alongside the likes of half-back Colin Veitch and left-half Peter McWilliam as Newcastle dominated the first years of the 20th century. With Association Football still in its infancy, Edwardian football had a style all of its own. It was not prac-

tice to catch the ball if you were in goal as is common today, but to punch the ball back out. Despite his popularity with both players and fans alike, Lawrence made two costly errors during his time with the Magpies, both in FA Cup Finals. He would end his St James' Park career having appeared in five FA Cup Finals (1905, 1906, 1908, 1910 and 1911) only once ending up on the winning side.

He was, however, a household name in the years prior to World War I, having taken part in three successful Championship teams (1905, 1907 and 1909) and five Cup runs. He was renowned for his antics in the dressing room and helped to keep morale high among team-mates with his pranks. However, he was also an intellectual and a keen football

politician. He became a leading figure in the Players' Union with his cool confidence. He was a godsend to the Union who were struggling to be taken seriously and was appointed to the Management Committee. Between 1921-22 he became the Union's chairman and was outspoken with the Football Association.

His football career began for Partick Athletic and Glasgow Perthshire, signing for United in July 1904. After leaving the club some 18 years later, Lawrence became manager for South Shields in May 1922 until the following January. After a two and a half year spell in charge of Preston North End, he moved to German club Karlsruhe as trainer in 1925 where his first season saw him take his new team to the regional division title. He returned to his native Scotland to become director at Stranraer before becoming chairman in 1933. He died in Scotland in November 1934.

League Championship

THE LAST TWO OCCASIONS Newcastle United picked up the League championship trophy, in 1992-93 and 2009-10, it was by winning the title in the second tier of English football. It is necessary to go back to 1926-27 to find the last season in which Newcastle United truly were crowned kings of England.

The Magpies joined the Football League when the Second Division was extended to 16 clubs in 1893-94 (Bootle resigned before the season kicked off so there were only actually 15 clubs competing for the title) and in their fifth campaign they finished runner's-up to Burnley to claim a place in the top flight.

They remained in Division One until the mid-1930s, claiming four titles. The first, in 1904-05, saw United pip Everton to the title by a single point as they registered 23 victories and two draws in their 34 League games. They also narrowly missed out on being the first team in the 20th century to achieve

the League and FA Cup Double when they lost the Final against Aston Villa.

Their second title came just two years later as players such as Colin Veitch, Andy Aitken and Bill Appleyard powered the Magpies to the First Division crown winning 22 and drawing seven of their 38 games. They won their third title in five years in 1908-09 with goalkeeper Jim Lawrence, on his way to setting a new record of 432 League appearances between 1904-22, keeping

17 clean sheets as Newcastle saw off the challenge of Everton.

They suffered relegation to Division Two in 1934 and were unable to regain their top-flight position until 1948, where they remained for 13 years. A second relegation brought a four-year spell in the lower league but the Magpies soared back to where they belonged claiming the Second Division title in 1964-65. United found scoring goals a problem in 1977-78 after selling Malcolm Macdonald – the most prolific striker in the First Division in two of the preceding three seasons – to Arsenal and were relegated.

They bounced back again in 1984 but only managed to retain their status for five seasons but the darkest moment was soon threatening. United went into their match on 2 May 1992 needing a win against Leicester City to guarantee avoiding the trapdoor into the Third Division for the first time in their history. As it was, Gavin Peacock and a Steve Walsh own goal gave the Magpies the result they needed and the following season saw them storm back into the top flight, winning the newly-renamed Division One title to claim their place in the Premiership.

League Cup

NEWCASTLE UNITED HAVE ONLY ever graced the League Cup Final on one occasion. Their route to Wembley in 1976 saw them overcome Southport, Bristol Rovers, QPR, Notts County and Spurs to set up a meeting with Manchester City.

The Maine Road club were enjoying a period of success in the 1970s, this being the third time they had reached the League Cup Final. Unfortunately, with a flu epidemic hampering United's preparations the week before, an Alan Gowling goal was not enough to bring the trophy back to St James' Park as Peter Barnes and Dennis Tueart (with a spectacular overhead bicycle kick) both netted for the Blues.

Other than this campaign, the furthest the Magpies have progressed in the League Cup is reaching the Fifth Round. They have found goals impossible to come by at this stage of the competition, however.

In 1974-75, they eliminated Nottingham Forest, QPR and Fulham before falling to Fourth Division Chester City by a 1-0 aggregate score over two legs. The other three occasions when they have narrowly missed out on a Semi-Final place were in 1995-96 (when they fell 2-0 to Arsenal), 1997-98 (Liverpool emerging 2-0 victors) and 2001-02 (against Chelsea when Jimmy Floyd Hasselbaink scored the only goal of the game).

BELOW Action during the 1976 League Cup Final

Lee

MIDFIELDER ROBERT LEE WAS born in Plaistow, East London on 1 February 1966. He joined the Magpies in September 1992 having signed from Charlton Athletic for a fee of £700,000. He began with Charlton as an apprentice turning professional in July 1983. During his 298 appearances for the club he scored 59 goals and earned himself the reputation for being one of the liveliest performers outside the top division.

His debut for United came on 23 September 1992 at home to Middlesbrough. His skills developed further and under Kevin Keegan and assistant Terry McDermott, Lee was instrumental in Newcastle's challenge for the Premier League title for several seasons following their 1992-93 promotion. When Kenny Dalglish took over following Keegan's departure in 1997, he showed great faith in Lee and gave him the role of captain.

But a lack of success saw Dalglish fired and Dutchman Ruud Gullit took over in the hot seat. Lee's relationship with the new manager was not without

ABOVE Robert Lee takes on two Wimbledon players

its disagreements behind the scenes and Gullit refused to even give his captain a squad number for the new season. He was also stripped of his captaincy and forced to train alone. However when Sir Bobby Robson arrived to replace Gullit shortly after his sacking, Lee was able to get back in the team along with team-mate

Alan Shearer who had also been out of favour.

Back in his number 7 shirt at the insistence of Kieron Dyer (who had been given the shirt by Gullit), Lee found his form as a strong defending midfielder who made opportunities for others to get forward rather than the attacking midfielder he'd been during the mid-1990s. Capped 21 times by England (scoring twice, the first time on his debut against Romania), Lee made a transfer request during the 2001-02 season when nego-

tiations over a new contract were rather slower than he would have liked.

By February 2002 he had signed for Derby County for £250,000. But his ten years on Tyneside had turned him into a Newcastle hero. The following year saw the Newcastle stalwart sold to West Ham by the Rams but he only got to play 16 games for the Hammers (the team he'd supported as a boy) and he was released on a free transfer, eventually signing for Wycombe Wanderers for the 2004-05 season.

Macdonald

MALCOLM IAN MACDONALD, THE centre-forward born in Fulham, West London on 7 January 1950, was one of United's most celebrated heroes. Signed by Joe Harvey for United in May 1971 for £180,000, Macdonald was known nationwide as 'Supermac', a phenomenon of 1970s football and a firm favourite with the Toon Army.

He began his playing career as a centre-back with Barnet and Knowle Park Juniors before moving to Tonbridge in July 1967 at the tender age of 17. He then joined Crystal Palace followed by a move to Fulham in August 1968. Signing for Luton Town in July 1969 for £17,500 where he scored 49 goals in 88 games, he joined United two years later making his debut for the Magpies on 14 August 1971 in an away game against his former club Crystal Palace. His St James' Park debut saw him register a hat-trick in a 3-2 victory against Liverpool and he topped the club's scoring charts for five consecutive seasons.

Supermac also made his debut for England against Wales while at Newcastle. Then in April 1975 he scored all five goals in a 5-0 victory against Cyprus – a record that still stands today. He became the third England player ever to achieve this feat and won a total of 14 caps for England but only scored once more for the national side. In all, Macdonald registered a better than one goal every two games strike rate, scoring 121 times in 228 appearances for the Magpies.

ABOVE Centre-forward Malcolm MacDonald in League action

forced to retire from the professional game at the premature age of 29 in July 1979 after suffering a knee injury in a match against Rotherham from which he never fully recovered.

Macdonald never won a major honour: the closest he came to a medal was appearing in two FA Cup Finals (in 1974 and 1978). Just prior to his retirement he did move to take part in Sweden's professional game for a short time, but his knee injury thwarted his career.

He returned to old club Fulham as manager for four seasons, and moved to Huddersfield Town between 1987-88. Supermac finally found his niche after professional football by becoming a commentator for the North East's radio station, Century FM, a columnist and after dinner speaker.

For an interesting fee of £333,333.33, Supermac moved to Arsenal in 1976, playing for his new club for two full seasons as their top scorer. However, he was

Managers

ONE OF THE LAST CLUB'S TO
appoint a full-time manager, Newcastle
United had been served by many illustrious names during their history.
From their formation in 1892 through
to December 1939, a selection committee would pick the team and no doubt
select the tactics, but as the club won
four League titles and two FA Cups
during that period, it obviously worked!

Andy Cunningham was appointed
manager on 1 January 1930 and would
win the FA Cup during his spell in charge,
a feat that would also be achieved by Stan
Seymour and Doug Livingstone. The
last manager to guide Newcastle United
to a major honour was Joe Harvey, who
helped the club win the Inter Cities Fairs
Cup in 1969. Here is the complete list of
Newcastle managers to date:

ABOVE Kenny Dalglish
after the Premiership
match against Chelsea
at St James' Park in
1998. Newcastle United
won the match 3-1

Name	From	To
Selection Committee	1892	1929
Andy Cunningham	1930	1935
Tom Mather	1935	1939
Stan Seymour	1939	1947
George Martin	1947	1950
Stan Seymour	1950	1954
Doug Livingstone	1954	1956

Name	From	To
Stan Seymour	1956	1958
Charlie Mitten	1958	1961
Norman Smith	1961	1962
Joe Harvey	1962	1975
Gordon Lee	1975	1977
Richard Dinnis	1977	1977
Bill McGarry	1977	1980
Arthur Cox	1980	1984
Jack Charlton	1984	1985
Willie McFaul	1985	1988
Colin Suggett	1988	1988*
Jim Smith	1988	1991
Osvaldo Ardiles	1991	1992
Kevin Keegan	1992	1997
Terry McDermott	1997	1997*
Kenny Dalglish	1997	1998
Ruud Gullit	1998	1999
Steve Clarke	1999	1999*
Sir Bobby Robson	1999	2004
John Carver	2004	2004*
Graeme Souness	2004	2006
Glenn Roeder	2006	2007
Nigel Pearson	2007	2007*
Sam Allardyce	2007	2008
Nigel Pearson	2008	2008*
Kevin Keegan	2008	2008
Chris Hughton	2008	2008*
Joe Kinnear	2008	2009
Alan Shearer	2009	2009*
Chris Hughton	2009	2010
Alan Pardew	2010	Present

McCracken

BELFAST-BORN FULL-BACK WILLIAM R McCracken made his debut for United in a home game against Woolwich Arsenal on 3 September 1904. Born on 29 January 1883, his career began at Distillery in December 1900 before being spotted by United. He also played as a war guest for Fulham between 1918 and 1919. Like other players of his generation, McCracken managed a long spell at St James' Park which didn't end until 1923, some 19 years after making his debut. He was still turning out for club and country after his 40th birthday.

Billy McCracken will be remembered as one of the most celebrated players in United's history and one of the most colourful characters. He will also undoubtedly be remembered for his tactics, being particularly skilful at playing the offside trap. McCracken was so adept at catching opponents offside that he constantly managed to frustrate both players and fans alike to the point where it was necessary to rethink the rules, which the football authorities duly did in 1925. They reduced the number of players who had to be between the attacker and the opponents' goal from three to two.

Despite his hero-status with United fans, he was often a controversial character in dispute with referees and other authority figures. His transfer to St

ABOVE Billy McCracken, a Gallowgate legend of the early 20th century

McCRACKEN

James' Park was also under scrutiny when rumours of illegal approaches and backhanders were rife. He partnered Frank Hudspeth for many years while at United despite having originally been second choice to Andy McCombie. However, he prospered with the club and was instrumental in helping the Magpies win three League titles and three FA Cups.

He was capped for his native Ireland a total of 15 times, and played a further two internationals during World War I. He made a total of 444 appearances for United, scoring eight goals before he became manager of Hull City in February 1923.

He stayed with Hull for eight years – steering them to an FA Cup Semi-Final in 1930 where they drew with Herbert Chapman's Arsenal before losing the replay by a single goal – before moving to Gateshead in September 1932. He also managed Millwall (May 1933 to March 1936), Aldershot (February 1937 to November 1949) prior to becoming a scout for United in September 1951 and Watford in January 1978. He died in Hull on 20 January in 1979, just short of his 96th birthday.

McDermott

MIDFIELDER TERENCE MCDERMOTT from Kirby, Liverpool joined Newcastle United on four separate occasions. Born on 8 December 1951, he started out as an apprentice for Bury, turning professional in 1969. He signed for United four years later for the fee of £25,000, but the following year was to see him transfer to his hometown side in 1974 costing £170,000.

He was to stay at Liverpool for eight years before heading back to the Magpies in September 1982 for £100,000. His playing career finished at Cork City (1985) and Apoel in Cyprus (1985-87) before he returned to St James' Park in February 1992 as assistant manager.

In his first season for United, having slipped through the net with his local teams, McDermott reached the FA Cup Final in 1974 but Liverpool claimed the trophy with a 3-0 victory. Within six months, however, new Liverpool boss Bob Paisley signed the young star after McDermott had a disagreement with United manager Joe Harvey. It was to take McDermott two years to

claim a regular place at Anfield and there was much speculation that his failure to progress would lead to his departure during the summer of 1976 but he stayed with the Reds and became an integral part of the team for the following season.

McDermott played 322 games for

ABOVE Glenn Roeder with coach Terry McDermott

OPPOSITE Bill McCracken

Liverpool, scoring 75 goals. His passing both short and long was exceptional and his goalscoring talents helped Liverpool to three European Cup victories. After Liverpool retained the Division One title in 1980, McDermott was voted the PFA Player of the Year and was also selected by England for the European Championships in Italy where he played in two games. He was not selected for the England squad for the 1982 World Cup in Spain and did not win any further caps.

McDermott returned to Newcastle in 1982 where he was instrumental – along with Chris Waddle, Peter Beardsley and former Anfield team-mate Kevin Keegan – in leading the club back into the top flight. But further disagreements at St James' Park saw the midfielder leave for Cork City.

He later returned to United as Keegan's first-team coach and he stayed on under Kenny Dalglish after Keegan's resignation but left when Ruud Gullit brought in his own staff. He once again returned to United in 2005 when he was recruited by Graeme Souness as coach and stayed on in February 2006 under Glenn Roeder.

McWilliam

LEFT-HALF PETER MCWILLIAM, born on 22 September 1878 in Inveravon, Banffshire, joined the Magpies in 1902 and spent the next nine years committed to United's cause.

Known as 'Peter the Great', McWilliam was an integral part of the team that won the title in his first full season at St James' Park. His talents at half-back were exceptional, with his famous body swerve designed and proven to outwit opponents. With eight caps for Scotland and 199 appearances and 11 goals for United, seven seasons with the Magpies made McWilliam a hit with the Tyneside fans.

A knee ligament injury – sustained in a match for Scotland – meant the end of his playing career, however, he went on to become a successful manager, backed up by his good tactical skills. He became Tottenham Hotspur manager in December 1912 and then Middlesbrough in January 1927 before becoming a scout for Arsenal

in the close season of 1934.

He moved back to his managerial position with Spurs in April 1938 and became one of the few to both play for and manage an FA Cup-winning side. Having received the Football League's Long Service medal in June 1939, McWilliam retired in June 1942 and died in Redcar on 1 October 1951.

ABOVE Peter McWilliam was on his way for trials with Sunderland when he was persuaded to join the Magpies

OPPOSITE Terry McDermott make notes during the Premier League game against Chelsea, 2006

Milburn

JOHN EDWARD THOMPSON Milburn was born on 11 May 1924 in the coal mining town of Ashington, Northumberland, 15 miles north of Newcastle. With reserved occupation status as a miner during World War II, it meant that the eventual Tyneside hero was confined to his home town.

Jackie signed for United in 1943 after writing to the club in response to their advert for trials in the North Mail newspaper. Arriving at St James' Park with a pair of borrowed boots, a pie and a bottle of pop, he made a huge impression and was invited back for the final trial match. The Stripes vs the Blues found the Stripes 3-0 behind at half time, but switching Milburn to centre-forward in the second half saw the young miner score six times as his side claimed a 9-3 victory.

Stan Seymour quickly signed him up for wartime League games while he

continued his job as a miner, but in 1946 when League football returned, Milburn soon became known as 'Wor Jackie' – the Geordie dialect for 'our'.

He went on to play 395 games for the Magpies and is still the second highest goalscorer at United with a staggering 200 goals. At first he played on the wing, but took up his role as centre-forward when Charlie Wayman left to join Southampton in 1947. He was integral in the club's victories

ABOVE Jackie Milburn celebrating after scoring against Blackpool in the FA Cup Final, 1951

throughout the 1950s when the club won the FA Cup three times in five years. Jackie also won 13 caps for England, scoring a total of ten goals.

He left the Magpies in June 1957 to become player-manager of Linfield in Belfast, becoming a firm favourite with the locals with more than 100 goals in just two seasons. He then managed Ipswich Town (1962-64) before returning to the North East to become a sports journalist for the News Of The World, reporting on the Magpies for more than 20 years. Ten years after leaving the Magpies he received a testimonial match which featured his nephews Bobby and Jack Charlton along with Ferenc Puskas, watched by a 50,000 strong crowd. Sadly, Jackie died at the premature age of 64 on 9 October 1988 from lung cancer. More than 30,000 people turned out to pay their respects at his funeral in St Nicholas's Cathedral in Newcastle. When the new West Stand was opened at St James' Park in the same year it was named after the hero who had scored a staggering 238 goals in 492 games during his career.

Mitchell

AS OUTSIDE-LEFT, ROBERT Carmichael Mitchell was a hero on Tyneside during the post-war era. Born on 16 August 1924 in Glasgow, Bobby Mitchell cost the club a record signing (£17,000) for a winger at the time, but his contribution to United's cause was to prove well worth the fee.

The former telegraphist for the Royal Navy during World War II began his professional career with Third Lanark in June 1942. He signed for United in February 1949 and made his debut against local rivals Sunderland at St James' Park on 5 March that same year.

ABOVE Bobby Mitchell, scorer of 113 goals in 410 games for Newcastle

OPPOSITE Celebrations after winning the FA Cup Final in 1951. Joe Harvey is with the trophy and Jackie Milburn, who scored both goals, is being congratulated by Ernie Taylor

Nicknamed 'Bobby Dazzler', Mitchell was tall and athletic with immaculate ball control and managed a total of over 100 goals for United during a career of 13 seasons with the club. He is currently joint-seventh in the list of all-time Newcastle goalscorers with 113.

He won three FA Cup winners' medals (1951, 1952 and 1955) and was renowned for raising his game for important matches. In the 1955 FA Cup Final against Manchester City, Mitchell was one of the goalscorers, along with George Hannah and Jackie Milburn.

His skills with the ball and his wing tactics along with contributing important goals for United during their games saw Mitchell as one of the greatest forwards that United have ever known. He was mainly in the team's number 11 shirt, but did have a short spell at

ABOVE Bobby Mitchell (centre) scoring Newcastle's second goal in the FA Cup Final against Manchester City in 1955

RIGHT Jackie Milburn and Bobby Mitchell arriving at Wembley for the FA Cup Final in 1952

left-half under manager Charlie Mitten.

He would have won far more caps for Scotland than he did, but Liverpool player Billy Liddell's skills often saw Mitchell overlooked, despite the fact that he scored on his debut in 1951. Sadly he was to win only two caps for his country despite scoring on his international debut. He was even the Scottish League's top goalscorer during 1946-47 scoring a total of 22 goals.

Following his time at St James' Park, Mitchell joined Berwick Rangers on a free transfer in June 1961 and was Gateshead player-manager between May 1963 and February 1966.

United held a testimonial match for him in 1961 which saw a large crowd of nearly 41,000 turn up, showing just how much the Scot meant to the Tyneside crowd. Mitchell retired from professional football in 1966 and went on to run two pubs in Jesmond and Heaton, becoming something of a local celebrity. He died in Backworth, Newcastle upon Tyne on 8 April 1993.

Nattrass

BORN ON 12 DECEMBER 1952 in Fishburn, County Durham, Irving Nattrass played at right-back for the Magpies between 1970-79. He began his career at United where he stayed for nine years before moving to Middlesbrough in July 1979 for a £375,000 transfer fee.

He made his debut for United in a home match against Derby County on 27 March 1971. He was originally a midfielder but later took over from David Craig as right-back before finishing his career with the Magpies in central defence. He was a refined player with the ability to stay calm and as a product of the club's junior ranks knew exactly the game he needed to be playing.

During his time at Newcastle he was awarded the captaincy, however, persistent injuries meant that a coveted England cap escaped him – he only won one England Under-23 cap. Injury kept him out of the game for some time – forcing him to miss the 1974 FA Cup run – and later dogged him for the remainder of his career.

When Newcastle were relegated in 1978, Nattrass joined First Division Middlesbrough where he made 220 appearances during seven seasons. After retiring from the professional game in 1986, Nattrass became a clothing retailer.

ABOVE Irving Nattrass made 313 appearances for the Magpies, scoring 22 goals

Owen

MICHAEL JAMES OWEN, BORN ON 14 December 1979 in Chester, began his career with Liverpool as an apprentice. With speed, acceleration and excellent striking abilities, Owen is one of the best footballers around. He has had a prolific career at both club and international level and was voted European Footballer of the Year in 2001.

Owen was instrumental in Liverpool's FA Youth Cup victory in 1996 and four months later signed professional forms. He scored on his debut against Wimbledon in May 1997 and soon became a first-team regular when Robbie Fowler was injured. During 1997-98, Owen was joint top scorer in the Premiership (with 18 goals) and was voted PFA Young Player of the Year. He grabbed worldwide headlines during the 1998 World Cup when he scored against Argentina.

His goalscoring for Liverpool was consistent and in 2001 he was an integral part of the club's most successful season for several years when the club won the League, FA and UEFA Cups. He moved to Real Madrid for £8 million in August 2004 in a part-exchange transfer with Antonio Nunez.

Owen's form for Real Madrid suffered as he was restricted to the substitute bench for much of the season. He moved to United on 31 August 2005 signing a four-year contract and his first goal for the Magpies came on his second appearance in a 3-0 victory at Blackburn Rovers on 18 September 2005. It was his club's first win of the season and he went on to grab a hat-trick in a 4-2 victory against West Ham later that year – scoring with his left foot, right foot and head.

A metatarsal injury in December 2005 in a match against Tottenham Hotspur

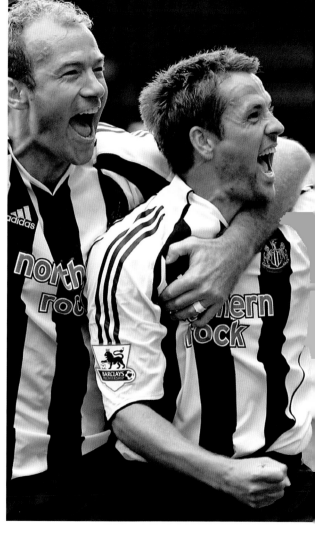

meant surgery to help speed up the healing process, but needed further surgery when that took longer than anticipated. He returned to the first team on 29 April in a game against Birmingham City.

Selected for the England squad for the 2006 World Cup in Germany, Michael suffered a damaged anterior cruciate ligament injury and would be out of action for nearly a year. The length of absence resulted in Newcastle threatening to sue the FA and FIFA for compensation, subsequently being paid in full to cover Michael's wages and other compensation. A succession of injuries, illnesses and niggles blighted his time at Newcastle, resulting in a return of 26 goals in 71 League appearances. Following the club's relegation in 2009, Michael signed for Manchester United on a free transfer, although his time at Old Trafford was to be punctuated by further injuries.

Pardew

THE APPOINTMENT OF ALAN Pardew as manager of Newcastle in December 2010 was not a universally popular one, his London roots drawing much criticism from the fans for what they saw as a continuation of the Cockney Mafia that had supposedly blighted their club for a number of years. Slowly, Ala won the detractors over, starting with a 3-1 win over Liverpool, some excellent performances and, more importantly, visible signs that the club was making progress on the pitch.

During a management career that had seem him in charge of Reading, West Ham, Charlton and Southampton prior to his arrival at St James' Park had seen him viewed as one of the bright young stars in the management game, but often having to perform miracles on shoestring budgets. Access to the greater resources at Newcastle represents the first major management role Alan has had during his career.

That steady progress saw the club flirt with the possibilities of Champions League football at the end of the 2011-12 season, with the club only just missing out on the coveted fourth place of the Premier League on the final day of the season. Still, fifth place meant qualification for the following season's Europa League, a much better finish than many sceptics had predicted at the start of the campaign. The protests that greeted his arrival are no more, replaced by hope and opportunism that Newcastle, and Alan Pardew, are truly heading for the stars.

Parker

SCOTT MATTHEW PARKER WAS born in Lambeth, London on 13 October 1980 and came to national attention aged 13 starring in a McDonalds television advert. The midfielder has represented England at every level from the Under-15s to senior level.

His career began with the FA's national school of excellence at Lilleshall, where he graduated before signing for Charlton Athletic, making his debut against Bury on 23 August 1997. In October that year, Parker signed professional terms for the club and despite only making sporadic appearances on the bench became one of the biggest prospects for English football.

He was loaned to Norwich City in October 2000 but within two months was back with Charlton replacing the injured Mark Kinsella. He also took over from Kinsella as captain the following season and soon won an England cap in Sven-Goran Eriksson's side.

He joined Chelsea in January 2004 for £10 million and was named PFA Young Player of the Year. Sold by Chelsea to United in June 2005 for £6.5 million, he has since found himself a first-team regular place. His form at United has been consistent, but he was diagnosed with glandular fever in March 2006 which ended his season and any hopes he had of making the 2006 World Cup squad.

RIGHT Scott Parker has found a new lease of life at St James' Park

BELOW Scott Parker receives the PFA Young Player of the Year Award, April 2004

Peacock

DARREN PEACOCK, BORN IN Bristol on 3 February 1968, made his debut for the Magpies against Norwich City on 29 March 1994. The country's most expensive defender began his career with Bristol City, Bristol Rovers, and Newport County before turning professional in February 1986. The young centre-half also went on to sign for Hereford United in a free transfer in March 1989 and Queens Park Rangers in December 1990 for £350,000 before eventually signing for United in March 1994 in a transfer deal costing the club £2.7 million.

It was his signing for United that earned him the 'expensive' tag in a record fee for the Magpies – a far cry from his humble beginnings with struggling Newport County. He had developed his skills at Loftus Road with QPR and quickly established himself as a capable defender. But it was United manager Kevin Keegan who was desperate to sign him and, after a persistent chase, the committed and determined Peacock joined the Magpies and gave the club a gritty stability with consistent ball skills.

He moved to Blackburn on a free transfer in 1998 before short spells with West Ham and Wolves, but was eventually forced to quit football in December 2000 after a blow to his neck which threatened his long-term health if he were to play again.

BELOW Darren Peacock has settled in Portugal following his enforced retirement

Quinn

RIGHT Watford's Glenn Roeder (r) jumps with Micky Quinn

OPPOSITE Micky Quinn finished his career with a total of 230 goals in 520 League appearances

KNOWN FOR HIS STOCKY BUILD, Michael Quinn was centre-forward for the Magpies from 1989-92. Born in Liverpool on 2 May 1962, Micky Quinn was a consistent goalscorer who started his career at Wigan Athletic before short spells at Stockport County and Oldham Athletic. However, it was during 1986-87 that he first gained attention as Portsmouth's leading goalscorer during their Second Division promotion campaign.

He was sold to Newcastle for £650,000 in 1989, making his debut in a home game against Leeds United on 19 August scoring four goals. Despite being the Second Division's top scorer, the Magpies lost in the play-offs. He went on to score a goal every other game for the Magpies and was the League's top scorer during 1989-90 and one of the few strikers to total over 30 goals in a single campaign.

During his career at United, the Liverpudlian made 132 appearances and scored 71 goals. He was sold to Coventry City for £250,000 in 1992 and scored 17 goals in his first season (ten of which were in his first six games). After loan spells with first Plymouth and then

Watford and brief forays abroad, he announced his retirement at the end of the 1994-95 season.

Quinn is now a professional racehorse trainer and commentator on racehorsing and football. Since 2005 he has written a column for the *Cambridge Evening News*.

Robledo

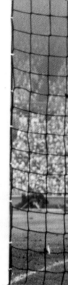

RIGHT The Arsenal goalkeeper watches helplessly as a header from George Robledo goes in

WITH YOUNGER BROTHER Ted as something of a makeweight to bring George Robledo to United (George wouldn't sign without his sibling), the pair signed for United in January 1949. The inside-forward was born in Iquique, Chile on 14 April 1926 to a Chilean father and an English mother and began his career with Dearne Valley Old Boys and Brampton Welfare before Barnsley amateurs in 1942 and Huddersfield Town amateurs in 1943. He joined Barnsley in April 1943 and appeared as a war guest for Lincoln City between 1943-44 before joining the Magpies in a deal for £23,000.

George Robledo was brought up in Yorkshire following the revolution in Chile in 1932 and became a pit worker at Wath. As an inside-forward he was also an incredible striker whose debut came on 5 February against Charlton Athletic. Stan Seymour was keen to bring Robledo to St James' Park and managed to sign the stocky player once United gained promotion to Division One.

Along with team-mates Jackie Milburn and Bobby Mitchell, Robledo became part of the club's formidable forwards. With a reputation for hard work and determination, Robledo was renowned for chasing after the ball, fearing no opponent, and was an excellent tackler and striker. He scored a vital goal to secure victory against

Arsenal in the latter stages of the FA Cup Final during the 1951-52 campaign and became the leading scorer (jointly with Hughie Gallacher) when he scored his 39th goal – this also made him the top division's highest goal scorer.

Robledo was also a hero in his native Chile as well as on Tyneside and won a total of 34 caps for his national side. At the age of 27, he was persuaded back to Chile to join Coco Colo in another joint deal with brother Ted, to develop the national game, later becoming a liaison officer and sitting on the organising committee when the World Cup was held in Chile in 1962.

He made a total of 166 appearances for United scoring 91 goals and is still the highest scorer of any one match with his record seven goals against Border Province (South Africa) in July 1952. George Robledo died in his native Chile on 1 April 1989.

His brother Ted tried to revive his career with a spell at Notts County (1957-58) and was reported missing overboard on a tanker in the Persian Gulf on 6 December 1970. The captain was charged with his murder and later acquitted but Ted's body was never found.

ABOVE Robledo shoots and scores past the diving Tottenham Hotspur goalkeeper in a Fourth Round FA Cup replay, 1952

Robson, Bryan

BRYAN STANLEY ROBSON, BORN ON 11 November 1945, led the line for United between 1962-71. Known as 'Pop', the boy from Sunderland was an astounding centre-forward and one of the most prolific goalscorers of his generation.

His career began with the Clara Vale Juniors before he signed for United in November 1962 for a fee of £75. Despite his successful club career, Robson never won a full England cap, but did win three caps for the England Under-23s between 1967-69.

While at Newcastle, the club won the Second Division title and the Inter-Cities Fairs Cup in 1969 when his partnership with Wyn Davies was instrumental in the victory. Although very much part of Joe Harvey's first team, it was not until Pop joined up with Davies that he began to find the back of the net on a regular basis.

Robson was sharp and quick and easily at home striking the ball from long distance as well as short range. After a disagreement with manager Harvey

over a lack of professionalism at St James' Park, Robson was transferred for a record £120,000 to West Ham in Feburary 1971 where he scored on his debut against Nottingham Forest.

He became the Hammers' leading scorer for two of the three seasons he spent at Upton Park and won the coveted 'Hammer of the Year' at the end of 1972-73. He then travelled north once again, but this time to join Sunderland for £145,000 in July 1974. However, two years later he was back with the Hammers

ABOVE Bryan Robson comes crashing down over West Ham United's Alan Stephenson

where he enjoyed another full season.

During his two separate spells at Upton Park, Pop made 254 appearances and scored 104 goals. He made the journey back to Roker Park, yet again, in June 1979 for just £45,000 where he took on the role of player-coach – later helping out at Carlisle and Chelsea. In 1982, Carlisle won promotion back to the Second Division where he teamed up with Peter Beardsley in attack. He was integral in keeping a struggling Sunderland from relegation when a 2-0 victory against Leicester ensured them of their Second Division status. He made 174 appearances and scored 67 goals for the Black Cats in his three separate stints with the club while his career statistics totalled 674 games and 265 goals.

Professional retirement saw Robson take up coaching, becoming assistant manager at Hartlepool, before becoming coach at Manchester United and youth team coach at Sunderland. He then became a coach for Leeds before becoming a scout for Birmingham City.

Robson, Sir Bobby

BORN ON 18 FEBRUARY 1933 IN Sacriston, County Durham, Sir Robert William Robson is known affectionately as the grandfather of English managers. Sir Bobby's love of football began when his coalmining father would take him to watch Newcastle United.

He began his own career at Fulham in May 1950 playing on the wing before he signed for West Bromwich Albion in March 1956. He made a total of 257 appearances scoring 61 goals while also winning 20 caps for England. However, in August 1962 he returned to Fulham before taking up the role as player-coach for the Vancouver Royals in Canada.

His managerial career began with Fulham, but he only stayed with the club between January and November 1968 before moving to Ipswich Town in 1969. It was with Ipswich that he was to establish himself as a successful manager where he re-shaped the side whose results consistently saw them in the bottom half of the First Division table. During the 13 years that Sir Bobby stayed with the club they were runners-up in the League on two occasions and won both the FA Cup and the UEFA Cup. He rarely brought in players from other clubs, preferring to develop the skills of the players who worked their way up through the youth team.

In 1982 he succeeded Ron Greenwood as England coach following the World Cup in Spain. The national team began to improve and he took them to the Semi-Finals of the World Cup in 1990 (where they lost to West Germany on penalties). His contract was not renewed by the FA and he moved to Holland to PSV Eindhoven and then to Sporting Lisbon in 1993. Porto appointed him after he was unexpectedly sacked from Sporting Lisbon who, under Sir Bobby, went on to win League titles in 1995 and 1996. Barcelona were keen to sign Robson and, after paying £12 million for Brazilian Ronaldo, went on to win the Copa del Rey, Spanish Super Cup and the European Cup Winners' Cup in 1997 –

with Robson himself being awarded the European Manager of the Year.

September 1999 saw Sir Bobby join his beloved Newcastle United where he guided them to a fourth place finish in 2002-03, third place the following season and qualification for the Champions League. He was dismissed on 30 August 2004 after a poor start to the season and on 13 January 2006 was appointed international football consultant for the Republic of Ireland. Five months later, Sir Bobby was revealed to be suffering from cancer, losing his life on 31 July 2009. He will be sadly missed throughout all football.

ABOVE Bobby Robson holds a Newcastle shirt in front of the assembled fans outside St James' Park

Roeder

BORN ON 13 DECEMBER 1955, Glenn Victor Roeder began his career as a defender at Leyton Orient before signing with Queens Park Rangers. In 1984 he signed with United where he notched up almost 200 appearances during his five years with the club helping them to the promotion from the Second Division in 1984. He spent a further two years playing for Watford and ended his playing career with Gillingham as player-manager.

In June 2005, Roeder was appointed as youth-development manager at United after nearly two years out of the game. In February 2006, when Graeme Souness was sacked as United's manager, Roeder was appointed caretaker manager with Alan Shearer as assistant. He successfully turned the Magpies around and they finished in seventh place in the Premiership securing a place in the Intertoto Cup.

Chairman, Freddy Shepherd wanted Roeder to take the role as manager officially, however, he was only half-way to gaining his UEFA Pro Licence, and Shepherd wanted the

FA to allow Roeder to continue without the licence. Early in May 2006, bound by UEFA rules, the FA rejected the request. But after much lobbying on the part of Shepherd, a press conference was held later that month and Roeder was officially unveiled as the Magpies' new manager with a two-year contract. In May 2007, it was announced that Roeder had resigned after an emergency board meeting.

Later that year he joined Norwich City, who were at the time bottom of the Championship.

Prior to his managerial role at United, Roeder spent one season as manager of Gillingham where he led the side to 13 wins in 51 games. He later joined Watford, at the start of the 1993-94 season, but was sacked in February 1996 while the side were struggling at the bottom of the First Division – his successor Graham Taylor was unable to avoid relegation. He spent the following five years as coach for both England and West Ham before taking on the role of manager for the Hammers in the summer of 2001.

Roeder suffered a brain tumour on 21 April 2003 and returned to manage the side at the beginning of the next season. A poor start in the First Division saw him sacked from his post in August 2003.

Rutherford

JOHN 'JACKIE' RUTHERFORD WAS born on 12 October 1884 in Percy Main, near Newcastle. As an outside-right, Rutherford served the Magpies between 1902-13. He signed for United in January 1902 for £75 making his debut at home against Bolton Wanderers on 1 March that same year.

Rutherford proved to be one of United's most outstanding forwards and, typically of all players of the Edwardian era, was devoted to the club for a number of years. His debut saw him score a goal, making him one of United's youngest scorers at the tender age of 17. Despite being a sound, confident and talented centre-forward, or inside-forward, he switched to the right wing during 1903-04.

By the age of 20 Rutherford had won several caps for England and eventually played for the international side for more than ten years. He possessed style, ability, speed and control which made him an invaluable asset. He became a firm favourite with the Gallowgate fans especially with his record of nearly 100 goals for the Magpies.

He eventually moved to Arsenal where he made more than 320 appearances. In 1919 he scored two goals for Chelsea before trying a stint in management with Stoke City as their first ever manager. Rutherford continued to play professional football into his 40s and later retired to London where he died on 21 April 1963.

BELOW A group of supporters in horse-drawn buses on their way to the FA Cup Final between Everton and Newcastle United, 1906

Seymour

GEORGE STANLEY SEYMOUR WAS one of the most distinguished men in United's long history. Born on 17 May 1893 in Kelloe, County Durham, Stan Seymour was associated with the club for nearly 50 years, having had teenage trials in 1909.

'Mr Newcastle', as he was affectionately known, was originally rejected by the Magpies and went on to join Shildon Town, Coxhoe and Bradford City in September 1911. However after many years with Greenock Morton he eventually returned to Tyneside as outside-left – a position he dominated – in May 1920 for £2,500. For eight seasons he was loved by the club and fans alike for his talents and goalscoring abilities.

Seymour was an integral part of the team that won the FA Cup and the Championship and he scored 18 goals throughout the title campaign. He retired from playing professionally in 1929 but returned to United some nine years later to sit on the board.

The club were convinced that Seymour had what it took to put some life back into the Magpies' game and to turn the club around. Seymour was in his element and quickly began to fashion the first-team line-up. His input proved invaluable and postwar, the Magpies were a roaring success throughout the country, much of which could be attributed to Stan Seymour. He died in his beloved Newcastle on 24 December 1978.

ABOVE Manager Stan Seymour with the squad in 1951

Shackleton

AS INSIDE-LEFT OR INSIDE-RIGHT, versatile Leonard Shackleton was considered one of the greats of English football. Born in Bradford on 3 May 1922, Len Shackleton served the Magpies between 1946-48 providing both excellent football and entertainment.

BELOW Leonard Shackleton served as an apprentice at Arsenal

His career began with local teams in Bradford before he joined Arsenal amateurs in August 1938. He then had several stints with other London clubs before returning to Bradford to join Bradford Park Avenue two years later. He had stints as a war guest with both Huddersfield and Bradford City before his signing for United in October 1946 cost the club £13,000.

His fee for United was a record at the time, but after his 217 appearances for Bradford and 171 goals was considered well worth it. In his debut for United at home to Newport County, Shackleton scored six goals out of the 13-0 victory that United registered on 5 October 1946.

However, despite Shackleton's exceptional form on the field, his relationship with management off it was another matter. He moved to local rivals Sunderland at Roker Park in February 1948 for £20,050 having managed only a season and a half with the Magpies. In his autobiography The Clown Prince Of Soccer one chapter is entitled 'The Average Director's Knowledge of Football' – the page is left blank!

Shearer

ALAN SHEARER OBE, BORN ON 13 August 1970 in Gosforth, Newcastle is widely recognised as one of the all-time greatest strikers in the history of football and is the highest scorer in United's history having netted 206 goals during his time at St James' Park. He is also the highest scoring striker in the history of the FA Premiership with 260 goals.

Originally rejected by United as a schoolboy, Shearer signed as an apprentice for Southampton aged 16, making his debut against Chelsea in 1988. One month later he made national headlines when he scored a hat-trick against Arsenal on his full debut. But despite his obvious talent, he only made ten appearances the following season, raising his profile in 1992 when he scored 13 goals in 41 appearances for Southampton. By this time, he already had a regular place in the England Under-21 team having scored 13 goals in just 11 matches. Graham Taylor gave Shearer his first senior England cap against France in February 1992 with the younger striker scoring in a 2-0 victory.

ABOVE Alan Shearer receives the Carling Player of the Month award, September 1998

Kenny Dalglish was keen to sign Shearer for Blackburn Rovers and paid Southampton £3.6 million. He became an England regular and went on to score 16 goals in 21 games for his new club. During the 1993-94 season he scored 31 goals in 40 games as Blackburn finished second in the table behind Manchester United – who had previously tried to sign Shearer.

ABOVE Alan Shearer celebrates scoring

RIGHT Shearer in action

The same season also saw him awarded the coveted Footballer of the Year.

When Chris Sutton arrived at Blackburn at the start of 1994-95, his partnership with Shearer was to prove magical and the pair were given the nickname 'SAS'. Shearer went on to score a further 34 goals from 42 games with Blackburn winning the title in the campaign.

Shearer ignored a further offer from Manchester United and moved to his home town when Kevin Keegan paid a staggering £15 million for his services following Euro 1996. He scored 25 goals in 31 games and at the end of his first season was once again awarded the PFA Player of the Year award.

His 30 goals from 63 England games put him level with Nat Lofthouse and Tom Finney although he decided to retire from the international scene in 2000. He was awarded an OBE in June 2001 and even though he announced he would retire at the end of the 2004-05 season he was persuaded to continue for a further season. On 11 May 2006 United held a testimonial for Shearer, although he couldn't play himself due to injury.

Solano

NOLBERTO SOLANO ORIGINALLY joined the Magpies from Boca Juniors in a £2.7 million move in 1998. Born on 12 December 1974 in Lima, Peru, Solano scored 29 goals in 172 appearances for the club and began his career with Alianza Lima before joining Sporting Crystal.

His obvious talents were spotted by Boca Juniors, the Argentinean giants where he was able to follow in the footsteps of Diego Maradona. In Peru, Solano became captain of the international side as well as his home country's most famous sporting personality becoming the first Peruvian to play in the Premiership.

Solano's passing and creativity with outstanding free-kicks have earned him a reputation of being one of the best. His talents are particularly awesome where he is most comfortable on the right of midfield. His most prolific position for Peru however is as wing-back.

During his first stint with United, a row over international commitments with Sir Bobby Robson saw the player sold to Aston Villa for £1.5 million in January 2005.

Then in August 2005, the Magpies brought Solano back for the same transfer fee just before the transfer window closed. Revealing that Alan Shearer had played a major role in arranging for his return, Solano would spend two years back at the club, making a further 58 League appearances. His one regret, he later stated, was that he was unable to help the club win a trophy during his time at St James' Park.

BELOW Nolberto Solano and Robbie Elliott in celebratory mood after scoring

Souness

BORN IN EDINBURGH ON 6 MAY
1953, Graeme James Souness has had
a prolific career both as a player and
manager. He began his career as an
apprentice with Spurs but was impatient with the lack of first-team chances
he received. In 1972, still a teenager, he
played in the North American Soccer
League for Montreal Olympique.

On his return to the UK he managed
one game for Spurs before moving to
Middlesbrough and in 1974 won his
first cap for Scotland. He was bought
by Bob Paisley at Liverpool in January
1978 for £350,000, following in the
footsteps of Alan Hansen and Kenny
Dalglish. The three Scots provided the
mighty Reds with the backbone to the
side that would dominate English football for the next seven seasons.

Souness was to become captain
of Liverpool and duly led his side to
two trophies the following season. He
made 358 appearances for Liverpool
and scored 56 goals while winning five
League Championships, three European
Cups and four League Cups. He also
made 54 appearances for Scotland and

scored four goals in 12 years.

He went on to join Rangers as player-
manager in 1987, but was sent off on his
debut for making two rough challenges.
He last played in the 1989-90 season for

Rangers and was renowned for signing English players for Rangers – something previously rarely heard of. He moved to Liverpool as manager in 1991 after Dalglish resigned, but for four years things were disastrous for the Reds.

In 1992 he underwent major heart surgery but was determined to lead his players out at Wembley for the FA Cup Final just days later. He remained with Liverpool until 1994 when he quit after an FA Cup defeat by Bristol City.

He went on to manage Galatasaray in Turkey but returned to England with Southampton. Differences with chairman Rupert Lowe once again saw Souness resign and he went to Italy to coach Torino Calcio for four months before moving to Portugal to manage Benfica. He became manager of Blackburn Rovers and took them back into the Premiership before winning the League Cup in 2002.

In 2004, Souness moved north to Tyneside where he took the manager's position with United. He found it a difficult time in the North East with poor form at the start of the 2005-06 season. He had hoped that signing Michael Owen for £17 million would turn the club's fortunes around, especially with an Alan

Shearer partnership. With team injuries and unrest among the fans, Newcastle were disappointingly in 15th place in the Premiership when Souness's contract was terminated on 2 February 2006.

ABOVE Graeme Souness gestures to his players

Speed

BORN ON 8 SEPTEMBER 1969 IN Mancot, Wales, Gary Speed is a midfielder, currently with Bolton Wanderers, who left Newcastle United in July 2004 for the relatively small fee of £750,000. He also captained his country until 2006 when he retired from international football.

His career began as a youth team player at Leeds United but he progressed to the first team and won the First Division title in 1992 before a switch to Everton four years later. Two years later, in 1998, Speed travelled to Tyneside to join United for the huge transfer fee of £5.5 million where he was to become a dependable midfielder. He was missed when he transferred to Bolton, but Sir Bobby Robson knew he would do well and had nothing but praise for the committed Speed. Giving him the highest accolade, Sir Bobby was reported as saying that Alan Shearer and Gary Speed were the best role models both on and off the pitch that he knew.

His talents on the pitch are particularly notable and his tackling skills are renowned. After retiring from playing internationally, Speed was urged by former international man-

ager Mark Hughes to apply to manage Wales…this position was eventually given to John Toshack who had alientated some of the players with his comments. Bolton manager Sam Allardyce, however, was keen for the midfielder to remain with the club for the remainder of his two-year contract.

Speed is noted for his total professionalism and his commitment to the game. He is known for giving 100 per cent. He made more than 280 appearances for the Magpies and played in two FA Cup Finals. Unfortunately, he was on the losing side both times: against Arsenal in 1998 and Manchester United in 1999. Speed's first season with Bolton was successful as he made 45 appearances and found the back of the net twice.

After four years with Bolton Gary wound down his playing career with Sheffield United, subsequently taking over as manager of the club in 2010. Four months later he was named manager of Wales, helping fashion as exciting a group of young players the country had seen in many a year. However, on 27 November 2011, he took his own life and sent the entire football community into mourning.

St James' Park

ST JAMES' PARK HAS BEEN THE home of the Magpies since 1892 when Newcastle East End took over tenure of the ground shortly before changing their name to Newcastle United.

When United joined the Football League in 1893, the ground boasted just one small stand but promotion to the First Division five years later and the success the club enjoyed during the 1900s provided the financial ability and incentive to upgrade the stadium. The new ground – dubbed Greater St James' Park – was officially opened by the Lady Mayoress on 6 September 1905 as United played host to Manchester City.

The stadium changed little throughout much of the 20th century as the club repeatedly fell foul of local planning officers. Indeed, when United proposed to erect floodlights in the 1950s, the council only agreed if they were switched off at half-time!

The arrival of Sir John Hall and the Premiership in the 1990s saw the ground extensively redeveloped. A staggering £42 million was spent on the Milburn (West) and Sir John Hall (Leazes) Stands to create the largest cantilever construction in Europe. A new bar was opened under the Newcastle Brown Stand at the Gallowgate End in 2005 that has been named Shearer's. In November 2011, the ground was officially renamed the Sports Direct Arena, a move that brought a wave of protest from the club's fans. To them it was, is and forever shall be St James' Park.

BELOW A view of the action from the FIFA 2002 World Cup qualifying match between England and Albania played at St James' Park

Stanley FC

THE SEEDS OF WHAT WOULD become Newcastle United Football Club were sown in November 1881 when Stanley Cricket Club formed an Association Football team going on to win their inaugural match against Elswick Leather Works 2nd XI by a respectable 5-0. A change of name to Newcastle East End was decided upon a year later to avoid confusion with other local sides and at the same time another local cricket club formed West End FC.

East End merged with Rosewood and played their home games at numerous grounds including Stanley Street and the Heaton Junction Ground while West End moved into St James' Park – a name that has become synonymous with football in Newcastle – in May 1886.

The two teams competed in local leagues and entered the FA Cup (West End in 1886-87 with their counterparts following suit a year later) before East End turned professional in 1889.

They became a limited company the following year but it was early in 1892 that dramatic changes happened.

West End were in financial trouble and approached their neighbours with a view to a merger. West End were actually wound up and East End took over the contracts of some of their players and backroom staff as well as the lease on St James' Park. On 9 December 1892, a near-unanimous vote confirmed a name change to Newcastle United, other suggestions being Newcastle City and Newcastle Rangers.

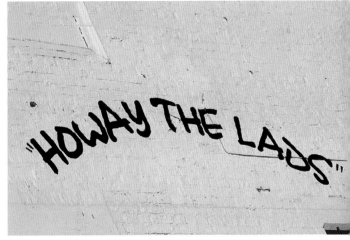

BELOW "Howay the Lads" on the side of the Strawberry Pub outside St James' Park

Stokoe

ROBERT STOKOE WAS born in Mickley, near Gateshead on 21 September 1930. He joined Newcastle as centre-half in 1947 and stayed 14 years with the club, signing in September 1947 for just £10 but his playing career was to take him into a prolific managerial role that started in 1961. He scored on his debut for the Magpies against Middlesbrough on 25 December 1950 in the number 9 shirt.

But Stokoe was impatient with the lack of opportunity afforded him by the club during his early years at St James' Park and made numerous requests for transfer, but a move to centre-half during the 1954-55 season saw him gain a regular first-team place. That same season saw United win the FA Cup. Stokoe made 288 appearances for the club and remained a stalwart for the Magpies until he left to become player-manager at Bury in December 1961.

His managerial flair was to see him lead Sunderland to win the FA Cup in 1973 and he enjoyed spells at Carlisle, Blackpool, Rochdale, Leyton Orient (as coach) and Charlton Athletic as well as becoming a scout for Swindon and Chelsea and a consultant for Bury before his death in Newcastle on 1 February 2004.

Texaco Cup

THE TEXACO CUP WAS A SHORT-lived competition that ran from 1970-75 involving English and Scottish teams who had not qualified for Europe. Following Texaco's withdrawal from the sponsorship of the competition, the name was changed to the Anglo-Scottish Cup in 1975.

Newcastle had their first taste of the Texaco Cup in 1971-72 but it was in the final two years of the competition that they enjoyed greatest success. The 1973-74 season saw Morton overcome 3-2 on aggregate to set up a meeting with Birmingham City. The two legs each ended 1-1 before the Magpies emerged victorious in a third match with John Tudor scoring twice in a 3-1 win.

Dundee United were the opponents in the next round a week later and although the Scots won 2-0 at Tannadice Park the Magpies eased through to the Final with a 4-1 victory at St James'. Goals from Malcolm Macdonald and Bobby Moncur gave United a 2-1 win after extra time.

The following season saw Newcastle retain their title beating Middlesbrough, Aberdeen and Birmingham en route to the Final. Southampton won the first leg 1-0 at the Dell but goals from Tudor, Alex Bruce and Paul Cannell in the return leg gave United a 3-0 victory and ensured the trophy remained at St James' Park.

BELOW The squad of 1975-76

Tiote

A TOUGH AND UNCOMPROMISING midfield player, Cheick Tiote provides the steel that has sometimes been missing from the Newcastle side in recent years. He is no push over and, by association, neither is Newcastle any longer. Born in Yamoussoukro in the Ivory Coast on 21 June 1986, Cheick played minor league football in his home country before being taken to Belgium and Anderlecht in 2005.

After two years progressing through the ranks Cheick was sent on loan to Roda JC on loan in order to gain first team experience, but in October 2008 was sold to FC Twente in the Netherlands, where his manager was Steve McLaren. There he was given an extended run in the side, a reward for his commanding midfield displays, which would ultimately earn FC Twente the League title at the end of the 2009-10 season. His performances had attracted considerable interest around Europe, with Newcastle paying £3.5 million in August 2010 to bring him to St James' Park.

The style of his play has both advantages and disadvantages. On the plus side, he seldom gives the ball away, has a near on perfect pass completion rate and is invariably on hand to win the ball back should it be required. However, his all action style also gets him into trouble from time to time, with his first 50 League matches for Newcastle seeing him collect 25 yellow cards, one every other game! Yet if that is the price of keeping Newcastle's midfield ticking over, then it is one Cheick is more than happy to pay. So much so, he has extended his Newcastle contract to 2017. 'The experience of playing in the Premier League has been better than I ever hoped it could be. This is a great club and the fans have been brilliant – I have never known support like it.'

Tudor

STRIKER JOHN TUDOR JOINED United in 1971 making his debut away to Burnley on 31 January after a professional career at Coventry City and Sheffield United. Despite being a good striker, his first campaign with the club was nothing special, but all that was set to change on the signing of Malcolm Macdonald (Supermac) the following season.

Born in Ilkeston, Derbyshire on 24 June 1946, Tudor began his career as an amateur for Middlesbrough and Ilkeston Town before joining Coventry City as an apprentice in January 1965. Three years later he turned professional and by November that same year he was signed for Sheffield. His transfer to United was as an exchange deal for Hope and Ford.

An intelligent player, Tudor found his career rocketed when Supermac joined the team and their partnership flourished over four successful seasons. The match was near perfect and many top partnerships since have failed to better them. Tudor was a dedicated and committed player who remained a stalwart for the Magpies until Supermac's departure and injury resulted in his own transfer to Stoke City in October 1976 for £30,000. An injury in the close season of 1978 saw him retire from playing, however, he went on to become a coach and then manager for North Shields.

BELOW Liverpool's Kevin Keegan tries an overhead kick past John Tudor in the 1974 FA Cup Final

UEFA Cup

APART FROM THE ANGLO-ITALIAN Cup success of 1972-73, Newcastle United's only other European title has been the Inter-Cities Fairs Cup in 1968-69. The predecessor of today's UEFA Cup, the Fairs Cup had been in existence since 1955 and was initially only open to cities that hosted trade fairs.

Newcastle's first opponents were Feyenoord and goals from Wyn Davies, Tommy Gibb, Pop Robson and Jim Scott gave the Magpies a 4-0 advantage to take to Holland (United lost the return leg 2-0). Sporting Lisbon were beaten 2-1 on aggregate before the Magpies drew 4-4 with Real Zaragoza but went through on the away goals rule courtesy of the two they had scored in the 3-2 defeat in Spain. Vittoria Setubal and Rangers were dispatched in the next two rounds to set up a Final meeting with Ujpesti Dozsa.

Bobby Moncur netted a brace as Newcastle won the first leg 3-0 and a battling performance in Hungary saw Moncur again on target, along with Preben Arentoft and Alan Foggon as

BELOW Alex Scott (third l) bursts through to score his team's third goal in the match against Ujpest Dozsa, 1969

the Magpies claimed the title with a 6-2 aggregate score.

The following season saw the St James' Park outfit ease past Dundee United, Porto and Southampton before going out on the away goals rule to Anderlecht, losing 2-0 in Belgium and winning the return 3-1. Inter Milan were beaten 3-1 on aggregate in 1970-71 before Pecsi Dozsa ended their interest in the competition winning on penalties after each side had won their home leg 2-0.

There were brief forays in the UEFA Cup in 1977-78 and 1994-95 before a sustained run in the competition saw them reach the Quarter-Finals in 1996-97. United knocked out Halmstads, Ferencvaros and Metz with Tino Asprilla scoring five times and Les Ferdinand contributing four goals over the three rounds to set up a meeting with Monaco. Unfortunately, Monaco proved impossible to crack and United lost the tie 4-0 on aggregate.

In 1999-2000, they reached the Third Round before being knocked out by AS Roma with only one goal scored over the two legs and four years later fell at the penultimate hurdle. Having beaten the likes of Real Mallorca (7-1 on aggregate) and PSV Eindhoven (3-2), United found themselves pitted against Marseille. The Magpies were unable to break down the French side and – after a goal-less draw at St James' – Marseille won 2-0 on aggregate.

Newcastle again reached the Quarter-Finals in 2004-05 and after Alan Shearer scored the only goal of the first leg against Sporting Lisbon, expectation was high for the return. The Portuguese dashed these hopes, however, emerging 4-1 victors in the second leg to leave Newcastle fans disappointed for yet another season. The club qualified for the Europa League (the successor to the UEFA Cup) for the 2012-13 season by virtue of their fifth place finish in the Premier League the previous season.

Upsets

ASK ANY NEWCASTLE UNITED FAN to name the biggest upset the club has suffered at the hands of lower league opposition and the majority will pick the events of 5 February 1972.

First Division Newcastle had entertained non-League Hereford United in the Third Round of the FA Cup on 24 January and were behind after 17 seconds. The rearranged game (postponed due to severe rain and snow) finished 2-2 with Malcolm Macdonald scoring a penalty and John Tudor netting the home side's second goal.

The replay at Edgar Street was again hit by the weather but eventually went ahead on 5 February in front of the Match Of The Day cameras. United, having missed several chances to open the scoring in the first half, went ahead through Macdonald but the Southern Leaguers equalised four minutes from time when Ronnie Radford scored from 35 yards. Although Ricky George became the Hereford hero when he netted the winner in extra time, it is always the Radford thunderbolt that is remembered and replayed on television

as Newcastle became the first top-flight team to lose to non-League opposition for 23 years.

Other notable giantkillings Newcastle have suffered while in the top flight include losing 2-1 to Fourth Division Lincoln City in the 1967-68 League Cup and 4-1 to Third Division Wrexham in the 1977-78 FA Cup.

BELOW Although Malcom Macdonald scored twice against Hereford, he was unable to prevent a giant killing

VENISON

Venison

BARRY VENISON MADE HIS DEBUT for the Magpies in a match against Southend on 15 August 1992 but his career had begun with Sunderland at Roker Park as a teenager where he made 206 appearances and became a star for the Wearsiders. He then moved to Anfield in July 1986 for £250,000 four years after signing professional terms, taking part in Liverpool's FA Cup victories in 1989 and 1992. Born on 16 August 1964 in Consett, Venison then joined the Magpies on Tyneside in July 1992 for a similar £250,000 fee.

Venison was instrumental in defence and masterminded tactics for other defenders from the right-back position playing an integral part in United's First Division championship success. His commitment and determination were gritty and he was just as comfortable showing off his ball skills and pace along with accurate passes as centre-half as he was in defence. His steely attitude earned him two England caps in the mid-1990s and the captaincy of the Magpies.

During his three years at St James' Park, Venison made 132 appearances for the Magpies before his move to Turkish team Galatasaray in June 1995 for £750,000 and subsequent signing for Southampton in October that same year for £850,000. He retired two years later through injury and now resides in America.

Waddle

CHRIS WADDLE GAVE UP A JOB AT a factory to join the Magpies in July 1980. Born in Heworth, Gateshead on 14 December 1960, Waddle made tremendous progress at St James' Park in a short time. Despite first appearances – it looked unlikely that he would be outstanding – Waddle went on to demand the third highest ever transfer fee after Maradona and Guillit later in his career.

Waddle, however, had immense talent that Kevin Keegan could see and wanted developed. He became renowned for his body-swerve and pace, fooling opposition defenders and earning himself a regular first-team place. It was during the Magpies' 1983-84 promotion season that Waddle really came into his own.

He was comfortable in the centre or on either wing and with Keegan and Beardsley also in the front line, United had a fearless trio of forwards. Waddle quickly established himself as a match winner capable of finding the back of the net, scoring 52 goals during his 190 appearances for the club.

Five years after joining United, Waddle was transferred to Spurs in 1985 for £590,000 and four years later joined Olympique Marseille in France for a then record of £4.2 million. In July 1992 he came back to the UK to play for Sheffield Wednesday before joining Falkirk in 1996 and Bradford City on a free transfer later that year. He retired in 1998 and has since become a regular radio pundit.

ABOVE Chris Waddle earned the nickname "Le Dribbleur Fou" during his time in France

Watson

BELOW Steve Watson in action during the European Cup Winners' Cup against Partizan Belgrade, 1998

STEPHEN CRAIG WATSON WAS born in North Shields on 1 April 1974. In July 1990 he became a United apprentice, turning professional almost one year later in April 1991. He made his debut for the Magpies against Wolverhampton Wanderers on 10 November 1990.

As the youngest ever player for Newcastle he proved a versatile player operating in midfield, as right-back, in central defence and in attack proving he could also comfortably become goalkeeper if necessary. His skills on the ball were renowned and his ability to find the back of the net were also spectacular. As an England Under-21 regular (he won 12 caps), he made almost 100 appearances for the Magpies before the age of 20. But he found his first team niche at right-back with his enthusiasm and energy making more than 130 appearances for the club and managing 12 goals.

He transferred to Aston Villa in October 1998, moving to Everton in the summer of 2000, becoming a regular for the club alongside Tomasz Radzinski. However, time with Everton saw Watson blighted by injury and he was signed by West Bromwich Albion before the start of the 2005-06 season. Turning down the chance of a further 12 months with Everton, Watson decided to team up with Bryan Robson's squad on a three-year contract.

X-Tra Time

WITH THE DEFEAT AT THE HANDS of Hereford in 1971-72, extra time has more often than not been unkind to Newcastle United. They lost a penalty shoot-out against Pesci Dozsa in the 1970-71 UEFA Cup and have also suffered three other similar knockouts in the League Cup.

In 1979-80 it was archrivals Sunderland who broke Tyneside hearts after their Second Round clash ended 2-2. Jim Pearson stepped up to take the 14th penalty knowing he had to score to keep United in the competition but it was Roker keeper Barry Siddall who turned out to be the hero. It was a similar story in 1998-99 when Blackburn Rovers held United to a 1-1 draw in the Fourth Round and then proceeded to win the penalty shoot-out 4-2.

They drew 3-3 with Everton in the Third Round in 2002-03 and the agony continued. Kieron Dyer and Nolberto Solano gave the Magpies a 2-1 advantage but Hugo Viana, Michael Chopra and Laurent Robert all failed to convert their spot-kicks and it was the Toffees who progressed to the next round.

Extra time has not been totally without success, however: in the 1998-99 FA Cup Semi-Final against Spurs, Alan Shearer scored twice to send Newcastle through to the Final after normal time had failed to produce a goal at Old Trafford.

ABOVE Kieron Dyer in action during a UEFA Champions League match

Youth Team

FORMER MANAGER KENNY DALGLISH is given much of the credit for the establishment of the current youth academy at Newcastle United having lured key staff from his previous club Blackburn Rovers. The club enter an Under-18 side into the Premier Academy League and the FA Youth Cup each season and supporters are invited to watch the home games free of charge at the Little Benton ground.

The FA Youth Challenge Cup has been competed for since 1952 and Newcastle United's youth team have twice claimed the trophy. The first victory came in 1962 when Wolves were defeated 2-1 while Watford were the victims of a 4-1 mauling in 1985 when a certain Paul Gascoigne grabbed the headlines.

Many youth team players break through into the first team and go on to become household names. The next generation of Magpies will be following in the footsteps of such St James' Park favourites as Gazza, Lee Clark, Shola Ameobi, Peter Ramage and Steven Taylor.

With former stars Kenny Wharton and Peter Beardsley currently empowered with coaching the youngsters, the future of Newcastle United seems to be in safe hands.

Zero

A LENGTHY RUN OF CLEAN sheets has not been that common in Newcastle United's recent history. When they met Wigan Athletic at the JJB Stadium in October 2005, they were looking to record their fourth consecutive shutout for the first time since the last few games of the 1996-97 season. As it was, a goal from Latics striker Jason Roberts proved to be the only successful strike of the game.

You have to go back to 1981-82 to find the last time that the Magpies kept more than four consecutive clean sheets in the League. That run started with a 1-0 victory over Barnsley on 6 March and finished with a 1-0 win away to Charlton Athletic on 3 April. Kevin Carr, ever-present in the Newcastle goal during that League

ABOVE Shay Given looks dejected during defeat to Wigan Athletic, 2005

campaign, prevented the opposition from scoring in 16 games during the season as the Magpies finished ninth in Division Two.

Of course, a lack of clean sheets can prove to be disastrous and this was very nearly true for the 1991-92 campaign. The club managed a miserly eight clean sheets as they battled against the drop to the Third Division. United only managed three clean sheets during the 1960-61 League season as they conceded 109 goals while surrendering their top-flight status.

ALSO AVAILABLE IN THE LITTLE BOOK SERIES

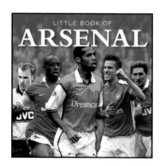

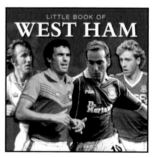

ALSO AVAILABLE IN THE LITTLE BOOK SERIES

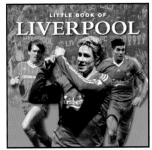
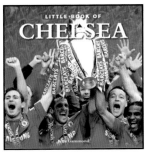
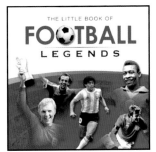

The pictures in this book were provided courtesy of the following:

GETTY IMAGES
101 Bayham Street, London NW1 0AG

EMPICS
www.empics.com

Design and artwork by Scott Giarnese

Published by G2 Entertainment Limited

Publishers Jules Gammond and Edward Adams

Written by Ian Welch and Claire Welch

Revised by Graham Betts